The Battle of Antietam
and the
Maryland Campaign
of 1862:
A Bibliography

Meckler's Bibliographies of Battles and Leaders

Series Editor: Myron J. Smith, Jr.
Series ISBN 0-88736-517-5

1. The Battle of Antietam and the Maryland Campaign
    of 1862: A Bibliography
    D. Scott Hartwig
    ISBN 0-88736-321-0   CIP   1990

2. The Central Pacific Campaign, 1943 - 1944:
    A Bibliography
    James T. Controvich
    ISBN 0-88736-325-3   CIP   1990

3. American Warplanes 1908 - 1988: A Bibliography
    Myron J. Smith, Jr.
    ISBN 0-88736-383-0   CIP   1990

4. The Battle of Pearl Harbor: A Bibliography
    Myron J. Smith, Jr.
    ISBN 0-88736-305-9   CIP   1990

5. The Battles of Coral Sea and Midway, May - June 1942:
    A Bibliography
    Myron J. Smith, Jr.
    ISBN 0-88736-683-X   CIP   *forthcoming*

6. Julius Caesar: A Bibliography
    Diane R. Gordon
    ISBN 0-88736-693-7   CIP   *forthcoming*

7. The Battle of Jutland: A Bibliography
    Eugene Rasor
    ISBN 0-88736-669-4   CIP   *forthcoming*

8. The Falklands/Malvinas Conflict: A Bibliography
    Eugene Rasor
    ISBN 0-88736-668-6   CIP   *forthcoming*

9. The Normandy Invasion, 1944: A Bibliography
    Colin F. Baxter
    ISBN 0-88736-557-4   CIP   *forthcoming*

10. Military Fortifications: A Bibliography
    Dale E. Floyd
    ISBN 0-88736-307-5   CIP   *forthcoming*

11. The War of Spanish Succession: A Bibliography
    W. Calvin Dickinson
    ISBN 0-88736-694-5   CIP   *forthcoming*

The Battle of Antietam
and the
Maryland Campaign
of 1862:
A Bibliography

D. Scott Hartwig

Meckler

Westport • London

Library of Congress Cataloging-in-Publication Data

Hartwig, D. Scott.
    The Battle of Antietam and the Maryland Campaign of 1862 : a
bibliography / D. Scott Hartwig.
       p. cm. -- (Meckler's bibliographies of battles and leaders ;
1)
    ISBN 0-88736-321-0 (alk. paper) : $
    1. Maryland Campaign, 1862 -- Bibliography. 2. Antietam, Battle of,
1862 -- Bibliography. 3. Maryland -- History -- Civil War, 1861 - 1865 -
Bibliography. I. Title. II. Series.
    Z1242.H37   1990
    [E474 . 61]
    016.973336--dc20   89-77215
                                                    CIP

British Library Cataloguing in Publication Data

Hartwig, D. Scott
    The battle of Antietam and the Maryland campaign of 1862 :
    a bibliography. - (Meckler's bibliographies of battles and
    leaders; v. 1).
    1. American Civil War. Maryland campaign - Bibliographies
    I. Title
    016 . 9737336

    ISBN 978-0-313-28071-9

Meckler Corporation, 11 Ferry Lane West, Westport, CT 06880.
Meckler Ltd., Grosvenor Gardens House, Grosvenor Gardens,
   London SW1W 0BS, U.K.

Printed on acid free paper.
Printed and bound in the United States of America.

To
Cindi, Jason, Lindsay, and Matt

Contents

Series Editor's Foreword

In *The Battle of Antietam and the Maryland Campaign of 1862*, D. Scott Hartwig has compiled a timely guide to the literature surrounding one of America's most famous — and tragic — Civil War military operations. Significant for its military aspects, including the battles at Harper's Ferry and Antietam, and its political ramifications, most importantly the Emancipation Proclamation, General Lee's September invasion — the first by the Army of Northern Virginia into the north — continues to attract widespread interest.

The scope of this work is comprehensive. The author cites books, memoirs, monographs, periodical/journal articles, documents, theses and dissertations, and several newspapers. Not only has he provided us with ample references on the campaign itself, but has included invaluable biographical citations and references to the many participating Rebel and Yankee units.

With such a variety of studies from which to select one or more specific or general topics or subtopics — along with a convenient campaign history and detailed subject index — the reader can quickly locate the most potentially pertinent or available material on this decidedly important military clash. Hartwig's study is the most comprehensive bibliography of this battle and campaign ever prepared. Students, researchers, historians, museum personnel, reenactment specialists, and Civil War buffs will benefit from this valuable reference work and I am delighted to see this title as the premier installment in Meckler's series of *Bibliographies of Battles and Leaders*.

Myron J. Smith, Jr.
Salem, West Virginia

Preface

The Maryland Campaign of 1862 was one of the pivotal campaigns of the American Civil War. It resulted in the largest capitulation of U.S. troops until World War II, at Harper's Ferry, and the bloodiest single day in North American history, the Battle of Antietam. In that one terrible day, September 17, 1862, nearly 25,000 American soldiers were killed, wounded, or captured. Of more significance than the military results of the campaign, were its political consequences. As a result of Lee's withdrawal to Virginia after Antietam, President Abraham Lincoln issued his Emancipation Proclamation, a document that changed the course of the entire war.

Given the significance of the campaign and its impact it would stand to reason that writing on the subject would have been prodigious. Surprisingly, this is not the case. Readers will find 688 entries in this bibliography. In contrast, Richard A. Sauers fine bibliography, The Gettysburg Campaign, contains over 2,700 entries. Sauers noted that since 1863 at least one study dealing with the Gettysburg Campaign, in whole or in part, has been written. In comparison, Francis Palfrey's The Antietam and Fredricksburg, written in 1882, was the only available study of the Maryland Campaign until 1965 when James Murfin published A Gleam of Bayonets.

Gettysburg, of course, was seen as a decisive battle, a turning point in the war. It was also a battle filled with controversy which fueled the pens of many of its veterans and produced an outpouring of articles and books. There was little controversy associated with Antietam. The battle was simply a grim slugfest with slaughter on a scale no one in either army had yet experienced in the war. Being a drawn battle, Antietam was not seen as a "decisive" battle either by its participants or post-war historians. As a result it never received the attention of Gettysburg.

There may be another reason why Antietam was seemingly slighted. Veterans may have found the battle a memory too grim to relive again on paper; slaughter with no purposeful outcome, where Gettysburg was seen to have resulted in more decisive results. That Antietam left searing memories is evidenced by one veteran of the battle, Lt. Colonel Rufus R. Dawes of the 6th Wisconsin, who wrote his wife during the Gettysburg Campaign after reading in a newspaper that another battle was anticipated at Antietam. "I hope not," Dawes wrote, "I never want to fight there again. The flower of our regiment was slaughtered in that terrible cornfield. I dread the thought of the place."

The entries in this bibliography principally concern the military operations of the Maryland Campaign and Battle of Antietam. A number of prominant general histories of the war were included as it was felt they would help round out how the campaign fit into the war. Also included were biographies of various general officers who served in the campaign. In the case of McClellan and Lee, the entries are obviously a handful of what has been published about these men, particularly Lee.

The most incomplete area within this bibliography is newspapers and manuscript collections. Since the emphasis in this bibliography was to be on published items only the largest collections of Maryland Campaign related manuscript collections were included. Newspapers were largely omitted simply because reading through all the major city newspapers would be impossibly time consuming. The newspapers that are covered are the National Tribune, a paper for northern veterans, the Philadelphia Weekly Press, and Philadelphia Weekly Times, both of which ran a series of Civil War articles in the late 1870's and 1880's.

Abbreviations for magazine articles was kept to a minimum. However, the following abbreviations were used.

SHSP - Southern Historical Society Papers
PWP - Philadelphia Weekly Press
CWTI - Civil War Times Illustrated

Each entry is assigned a number for use with the index. The vast majority of entries are annotated. The purpose is to provide some clue as to the volume's value in regards to the Maryland Campaign and, if not stated in the title, to identify what unit the author served with.

A number of bibliographies were consulted in preparing this bibliography. These, plus others, are listed in Chapter 3. The National Tribune articles were tediously compiled over a period of several years by the compilier. Although an index for this newspaper is available, it does not contain all the articles published in the newspaper.

It goes without saying that I have probably not uncovered everything ever published on the Maryland Campaign. If readers are aware of items not included in this bibliography I encourage them to write.

My ultimate hope in producing this bibliography is to provide a useful reference for further study and scholarship on this signally important campaign of the American Civil War.

1.
The Battle of Antietam
and the Maryland Campaign:
A Survey

    Following the defeat of the Federal army at 2nd Manassas,
Confederate General Robert E. Lee determined to maintain the
initiative and keep the Federal armies off balance by
invading Maryland with his Army of Northern Virginia. Great
possibilities beckoned from the border state. A convincing
defeat of the Federal Army of the Potomac on northern soil
could have a profound impact upon whether England or France
recognized the young Confederacy, and directly affect the
upcoming congressional elections. Lee's army was also in
desperate need of supplies, and Maryland's untouched, fertile
fields offered food and forage in abundance.
    After three months of active campaigning and a series of
bloody battles, the Army of Northern Virginia was in pitiable
condition. Many were barefoot, uniforms were in rags and
regiments that had once numbered 1,000 men were reduced to
less than 100. The army was in no condition to mount an
invasion into enemy territory, but Lee, ever the calculated
gambler, sensed an opportunity was being offered that must be
seized, and believed the risk was worth the potential gain
of bringing the war to an early conclusion.
    With approximately 55,000 men of all arms, supported by 246
guns, Lee turned his divisions northward. At this point of
the war the largest combat formation permitted by law in the
Confederacy was a division. Lee had discovered that one man
could not control a large number of divisions during the
clumsily fought battles on the Peninsula. Following the Seven
Days battles he grouped his divisions into two wings,
essentially corps, under Major General James Longstreet and
Major General Thomas J. "Stonewall" Jackson. These formations
were loosely organized, Lee assigning and detaching divisions
at will depending upon the mission of the corps, and even as
the army entered Maryland the organization of the army was
still taking place. During the army's operations in Maryland
it contained 9 divisions, 4 under Jackson and 5 with
Longstreet, although this arrangement was not closely adhered

to. A cavalry brigade under Major General James E. B. "Jeb"
Stuart and an artillery reserve rounded out the army. It was
a veteran army and was imbued with an agressive spirit,
confidence in its ability to deliver victory, and unflinching
faith in its leadership.

Between the 4th and 7th of September, Lee's army splashed
across the Potomac River above Leesburg, Virginia, into
Maryland. Lee chose to cross east of the Blue Ridge
mountains, rather than west of the mountains, in the belief
that by crossing east of the mountains he would threaten
Baltimore and Washington and force the federals to react to
his invasion.

The army concentrated at Frederick, Maryland, where Lee
allowed his weary regiments a badly needed rest, and he could
study the reaction of the federal army, and the state of
Maryland, to his invasion.

Maryland's reaction was disappointing but not unexpected.
Few of the Bay Staters displayed elation at the arrival of
the southern host, indeed, the reception in many towns and
villages was sullen and Unionist in sentiment. Lee published
a proclamation on September 8th, outlining his army's
purpose, to calm Marylanders fears and assure them his troops
would assist them in "throwing off the foreign yoke" that
gripped their land. By September 9th, Lee could delay his
movements no longer. Maryland had greeted his proclamation
with indifference and there was reluctance on the part of
Maryland farmers and merchants to accept Confederate money
for food and forage. Lee now planned to move his army west of
the South Mountain Range and hopefully into Pennsylvania,
drawing the federal army far from their base of supply, where
they could be destroyed. In planning this movement Lee
anticipated the federal garrisons at Harper's Ferry and
Martinsburg, Virginia would be abandoned once his army
entered Maryland. They were not. Sitting astride Lee's
proposed line of communications down the Shenandoah Valley,
the garrisons could not be ignored.

In a typical display of the caculated audacity that marked
his successful generalship, Lee devised a bold plan to
capture these federal garrisons. Three seperate columns,
under the command of Jackson, would descend upon Harper's
Ferry from three directions, bottling up the garrison and
forcing its surrender. A fourth column, under Longstreet and
accompanied by Lee, would halt near Boonsboro where it could
cover the army's rear and lend support to Jackson if
necessary. The cavalry would screen the army's movements.
Special Orders No. 191 was drawn up detailing the various
movements of Lee's plan and distributed to the principal
commanders involved. The following day, September 10, the
army was put in motion and the occupation of Frederick came
to an end.

On September 7th, the Federal Army of the Potomac took the
field to drive the southern invaders from Maryland. It was
composed of 16 divisions organized into 5 army corps and an
independent division numbering approximately 74,000 men.

On paper it was a formidable force, but in reality it was not
the equal of the Army of Northern Virginia. Its commander,
Major General George B. McClellan, did not enjoy the
confidence of the administration and had been placed in
command only with great reluctance on the part of Lincoln.
Slightly one year earlier, McClellan had been called from a
successful campaign in western Virginia to take command of
the beaten federal army from 1st Manassas. The young,
handsome general, styled the "Young Napoleon," displayed
organizational brilliance in forging what he named the Army of
the Potomac. It was the most well-disciplined and equipped
army the nation had ever produced.

After a long fall and winter of inactivity, McClellan
embarked upon an ambitious and imaginative plan to tranfer
his army by water to the Virginia Peninsula, and move upon
Richmond. Although well conceived, the campaign was poorly
executed by McClellan. He routinely overestimated enemy
strength, hesitated to act, and magnified his difficulties.
In every instance where he encountered the Confederate army
in battle, although he possessed the larger army, he was
outnumbered at the point of contact. Ultimately, his campaign
met ignominious defeat at the hands of Robert E. Lee in a
series of confusing battles called the "Seven Days Battles."

McClellan managed to halt his retreat at Harrison's
Landing, on the York River. Recovering his shaken composure
he sent forth new requests for reinforcements and even
paused to write Lincoln on how the war should be conducted.
Publicly, Lincoln did not waver in his support of
McClellan, but privately he admitted the general was "good
for nothing for an onward movement."

The military situation by July was such that Lincoln felt
the need for professional military advice. He therefore
summoned Major General Henry W. Halleck, a prominant general
from the western theater, to take the post of General-in-
Chief. Halleck arrived in Washington on July 23rd, and the
next day embarked for the Peninsula to meet with McClellan,
armed with instructions that if the general would not take
the offensive with the reinforcements the administration was
willing to offer, he would be withdrawn. McClellan
reluctantly agreed to the administration's offer, but after
Halleck's return to Washington he changed his mind and
renewed his request for huge reinforcements. On August 4th,
Halleck ordered the army withdrawn from the Peninsula.
McClellan sent up a howl of protest, but the order stood.

It was Halleck's intention to combine McClellan's army
with Major General John Pope's Army of Virginia, which had
been organized to operate against Richmond via the overland
approaches. However, Lee moved swiftly to prevent this
junction from being made. Leaving an observation force to
keep an eye on McClellan's army, Lee moved against Pope with
the bulk of his army.

McClellan's position, once the two armies were combined,
was kept deliberately vague, for the administration hoped
that if Pope was successful against Lee, McClellan could be
quietly disposed of without protest from his powerful
Democratic Party friends. As units of the Army of the Potomac

disembarked in Northern Virginia, they were hustled off to
Pope and temporarily detached from McClellan's command.
McClellan's future looked gloomy. "I take it for granted that
my orders will be as disagreeable as it is possible to make
them," he wrote his wife, "unless Pope is beaten, in which
case they will want me to save Washington again."

On August 28th elements of Pope's army collided with
Jackson's command near the old 1st Manassas battleground.
The following day a furious battle developed as Pope
attempted to destroy Jackson's isolated command. In
Washington, Pope's situation was disturbingly vague. His
communications had been cut by Jackson on the 26th and Henry
Halleck had little idea of how Pope was faring. To restablish
communications and reinforce Pope, on the morning of the
27th, Halleck ordered McClellan to march the 6th Corps at
once in the direction of Centreville, Virginia. McClellan
was in Alexandria, Virginia where he had proceeded to at
Halleck's request to assume direction of affairs there.
Essentially, he was fufilling the role of a staff officer,
simply seeing that men and supplies were forwarded without
delay to Pope. The 6th Corps was under McClellan's
operational control, and he hestitated to obey Halleck's
order. The situation in the direction of Manassas was
entirely too uncertain for McClellan's cautious mind to risk
sending a fine army corps into. Eventually, after Halleck
issued premptory orders, Franklin marched, but the entire
incident was seen as a deliberate act by McClellan to withold
support from Pope.

On the 29th yet another incident caused McClellan to be
caught up in controversy. When Lincoln sent to him for news,
McClellan replied with advice that the government should
either "concentrate all our available forces to open
communications with Pope," or, "leave Pope to get out of his
own scrape, and at once use all our means to make the
capital perfectly safe." His choice of words shocked and
angered the President, who shared the opinion of others that
McClellan wished Pope to fail.

The initial news from Pope was optimistic, but it turned
sour on August 30th, when it became evident that the army had
suffered a reverse. That night, utterly exhausted by the
enormous pressure, Halleck telegraphed McClellan requesting
his assistance. The following morning Halleck verbally placed
McClellan in command of the capital's defenses. Throughout
the day the gravity of the situation towards Manassas
developed, and it became apparent Pope had suffered a heavy
defeat, and the entire army was retiring upon Washington.
Lincoln sensed the need for someone who knew the capital's
defences well and could reorganize the defeated army.
Despite grave misgivings, he realized that McClellan was
his only logical choice. On the morning of September 2d, he
placed the Pennsylvanian in command of all forces within the
fortifications. It was Lincoln's intention to utilize
McClellan's superior organizational talents to make the army
field worthy again while he shopped about for a new field
commander. However, Lee made it imperative that Lincoln
select a field commander and organize a field army by

invading Maryland.

The President turned to Major General Ambrose Burnside, who had made a fine record in combined operations along the North Carolina coast, but the Rhode Islander turned Lincoln's offer down. Halleck was unwilling to assume field command and the army would not serve again under Pope. Lincoln saw no alternative but to restore McClellan, and on the morning of the 6th verbally placed him in command of the army in the field.

McClellan went to work immediately organizing an army to meet Lee. He selected the 2d and 6th corps of his Peninsula Army, the 1st and 12th Corps of Pope's Army of Virginia, Burnside's 9th Corps, Couch's Division of the 4th Corps and Sykes Division of U.S. Regulars from the 5th Corps. McClellan grouped these various formations into three informal "wings". The right wing consisted of the 1st and 9th Corps and was placed under the command of Burnside. The left wing contained the 2d and 12th Corps and was commanded by Major General Edwin V. Sumner, an officer of great experience but mediocre talents. Major General William B. Franklin, an intelligent but unenergetic soldier, led the 6th Corps and Couch's Division. Sykes Division was held by McClellan as an army reserve.

A cavalry division was also organized and placed under the command of Brigadier General Alfred Pleasonton, an officer of limited ability. Although on paper Pleasonton's division contained five brigades, these were administrative more than tactical, for in actual practice the cavalry regiments were parceled out to infantry commands, or detached to guard trains or serve as escorts. Consequently, Pleasonton never employed more than two or three regiments against the Confederates at any one point. Because of this, he would be unable to penetrate the cavalry screen Jeb Stuart maintained, thus limiting the amount and accuracy of the intelligence information he passed on to McClellan.

Union artillery was also in dismal condition. There was no uniformity in how batteries were assigned in the various Union Corps. One corps grouped all their batteries, another assigned its informally to the infantry brigades, while others assigned them to the divisions. The result was that the artillery strength of the army was dissipated, and only with great effort could a large amount of guns be concentrated at one point. The splendid artillery reserve was largely broken up during the withdrawal of the army from the Peninsula and only 7 of its original 18 batteries remained. McClellan attempted to address the condition of his artillery by naming Brigadier General Henry Hunt as his chief of artillery. Hunt made some changes, but a major reorganization while the army was on the march was impossible, and the army fought the battle of Antietam with an inefficient artillery organization.

To bolster the ranks of the infantry, over 20 new regiments, largely composed of raw recruits with little or no training, were assigned to the army. This represented close to 16,000 men, or about twenty per-cent of McClellan's infantry. The balance of the army's infantry was veteran

although morale was generally bad, and in some corps and
divisions, discipline was loose.

The condition of his army strongly influenced McClellan's
strategy during the campaign. His general goal was to push
Lee out of Maryland but to avoid engaging the Confederates in
a pitched battle.

The army sortied forth from Washington on September 7th.
McClellan moved it by short marches to allow the process of
reoranization to proceed and give his many new recruits some
seasoning. Pleasonton's cavalry quickly made contact with
Stuart's cavalry screen, but was unable to penetrate it, and
Lee's strength and intentions remained a mystery to McClellan
for several days.

As the Army of the Potomac cautiously felt its way across
Maryland, Lee's veterans were descending upon Harper's Ferry.
By the 13th, the federal garrison there was bottled up by
Jackson, Walker and McLaws' commands, and the post's surrender
seemed imminent. But the operation had run behind schedule,
and by a freak incident, Lee's widely seperated army was
suddenly exposed to grave danger.

On September 12th, the Army of the Potomac occupied
Frederick, pushing Stuart's cavalry out of the city in a
small skirmish. McClellan was still ignorant of Lee's purpose
but believed his army to number 120,000. The following day,
the foggy picture was instantly cleared by a remarkable
discovery, made by two non-commissioned officers of the 27th
Indiana Infantry of the 12th Corps. The regiment had arrived
on the outskirts of the city at about noon. Moments after the
regiment had halted, a sergeant and corporal of the regiment
discovered a piece of paper wrapped around three cigars. The
paper proved to be a copy of Special Orders No. 191 addressed
to D. H. Hill, from Army of North Virginia Headquarters.
Within minutes, the order was in McClellan's hands. The
opportunity was one few commanders have ever enjoyed. The
movements of every element of Lee's army were spelled out.
McClellan had only to act promptly to deal Lee's dispersed
army a smashing blow. "...If I cannot whip Bobby Lee, I will
be willing to go home," he remarked to one officer, waving
the copy of S.O. no. 191 in the air.

Despite the need for urgent action and McClellan's
boastful confidence, he did not act. Not until 6 P.M. did he
issue any orders. The army was ordered to march, not that
afternoon, but the next morning. And so, the opportunity of a
lifetime was squandered.

McClellan's plan for September 14th was to break Lee's
center. Franklin's 6th Corps, reinforced by Couch's Division,
was ordered to march at daylight and force Crampton's Gap, on
the road to Harper's Ferry. The remainder of the army would
march on the National Turnpike, cross Turner's Gap and
interpose themselves between Lee, at Boonsborough, and his
forces besieging Harper's Ferry.

Lee had received warning that the federal army was
approaching more rapidly than anticipated and that the
Harper's Ferry operation was encountering delays. Against
the advice of Longstreet, Lee decided to march to Turner's
Gap on the morning of the 14th with Longstreet's command, and

reinforce D. H. Hill's Division, which was positioned at
Boonsborough and had been ordered to defend the mountain
gaps.

Early on the 14th, elements of Pleasonton's cavalry,
supported by a division of the 9th Corps, started forward to
clear Turner's Gap, through which ran the National Turnpike.
The pass proved to be occupied by the Confederates in force,
so the federals moved to outflank the gap by advancing up the
Old Sharpsburg Road to Fox's Gap. The federals encountered a
brigade of D. H. Hill's Division and the Battle of South
Mountain was on.

The battle stumbled on through the morning. Hill was
sorely pressed, and had McClellan started his troops at an
earlier hour, or the night before, Turner's Gap would surely
have fallen. Instead, Hill was able to hold on by his
fingernails and be reinforced by Longstreet during the early
afternoon. By the late afternoon, the Union 1st and 9th
Corps were at last in position to launch a coordinated
attack, it having taken most of the day to get the troops up
and in position. The Confederate defenders were stretched
thin at nearly every point and when the blow fell, there was
little hope in stopping it. At Fox's Gap, heavy fighting
raged from mid-afternoon until nearly dark. Although the
southern defenders suffered heavy losses, the 9th Corps was
unable to seize and hold the summit of the gap.

North of Turner's Gap, Hooker's 1st Corps overwhelmed
several southern brigades in sharp fighting and by nightfall
held a position that completely dominated Turner's Gap. Union
losses in the day's action had been 1,813, while Confederate
losses totalled approximately 1,950, including over 600
prisoners. Tactically, the battle had been a Union victory.
Strategically, and more importantly, it had been a southern
victory. Lee had gained a precious day and prevented
McClellan from interposing his force between Lee and
Jackson's force.

Several miles south of Turner's Gap, General Franklin's
6th Corps had encountered greater success in its efforts to
force Crampton's Gap. Franklin's leading elements reached the
village of Burkittsville, approximately one mile east of
Crampton's Gap, around noon. They discovered Crampton's and
Brownsville Pass, one mile south of Crampton's, were both
held in some force. Franklin allowed the remainder of his
corps to come up and paused to study the approaches and
develop a plan of attack.

Actually, the Confederate defenders were pitifully few.
Two small regiments of cavalry, a severely understrength
infantry brigade, and some artillery, about 600 men maximum,
were all that stood in the path of Franklin's 12,000 men.
Yet, so boldly did they stand their ground that they deceived
the federals into believing the pass was strongly held.

Around mid-afternoon, after much deliberation, Franklin
moved to the attack. The attack stalled before accurate
musketry fire. Franklin's confidence began to wane, and he
contemplated calling off the assualt, when his front line
brigadiers led their men in a surging charge. The attack
struck the Confederates as their ammunition was giving out

and drove them pell-mell up the side of the mountain.

As the Confederate retreat was commencing, Brigadier General Howell Cobb's Brigade arrived to reinforce Crampton's defenders. His men met the relentless federal assualt and were simply overwhelmed. The southern retreat turned into a full rout with the survivors running down the western slope of the mountain. By sunset, Crampton's Gap was securely in Franklin's hands. The 6th Corps had lost 533 men in the battle, while Confederate losses totalled nearly 2,200, many of this number being prisoners.

Unfortunately for Franklin, he had commenced his attack so late in the day he was unable to follow up his success and contented himself with consolidating his position at Crampton's.

When Major General Lafayette McLaws learned of the Union breakthrough in his rear, he reacted immediately with decisive action. Under the cover of night he assembled four fresh brigades and reformed the two shaken brigades from the Crampton's fight. By morning he had a line of perhaps 4,000 infantry, strongly supported by artillery, stretching across the floor of Pleasant Valley.

The events of September 14th shook Lee's confidence. The setbacks of the day combined with the fact that nothing had been heard from Jackson prompted Lee to prepare for a withdrawal from Maryland. McLaws was instructed to locate a ford over the Potomac and cross into Virginia. The forces with Lee would retire to Virginia via Sharpsburg.

Under the cover of darkness, Longstreet and Hill's commands extricated themselves from South Mountain unmolested and commenced their retreat. Enroute Lee changed his mind about retiring immediately and ordered the march to halt at Keedysville, where he could lend some support to McLaws in his efforts to retire. Upon reflection, Lee changed his mind and decided to make his stand at Sharpsburg rather than Keedysville.

As his weary troops plodded across the stone bridge, that carried the Boonsborough Pike into Sharpsburg, during the early morning of September 15th, Lee received news from Jackson that Harper's Ferry surrender was imminent. The strategic picture was suddenly dramatically changed and Lee saw an opportunity to salvage his campaign if he could reunite his army before McClellan struck a blow. Counting upon McClellan's characteristic caution, Lee planned to make a bold show of strength with his three slim divisions until Jackson, Walker and McLaws could rejoin him at Sharpsburg. This was undoubtably one of the boldest decisions of Lee's career, for the odds were tremendous. His three available divisions and artillery did not exceed 15,000 men, while McClellan could bring four corps and one division, over 60,000 men, against him.

When daylight broke on South Mountain, McClellan's skirmishers advanced and discovered the Confederates had withdrawn during the night. A rather clumsy pursuit was organized and the army proceeded after Lee. In McClellan's mind he had dealt the Confederates a heavy blow, and fully anticipated Lee would withdraw from Maryland. It appeared

McClellan's strategy had been successful. He had avoided a pitched battle against the full strength of Lee's army and had succeeded in ridding Maryland of its invaders.

Around noon, while riding over the battleground at Fox and Turner's Gap, McClellan received word that the southern forces had halted behind Antietam Creek and were deployed to dispute its crossing. Surprised by this unexpected development, McClellan rode immediately to the front. Any attack upon Lee's position that day was out of the question. It would take most of the day simply to march the four corps and Sykes Division from South Mountain to the vicinity of Keedysville. McClellan therefore contented himself with studying Lee's position across the Antietam and seeing to the disposition of his arriving corps.

Meanwhile, in Pleasant Valley, General Franklin had discovered McLaws' six brigades stretched across Pleasant Valley. He occupied most of the morning in studying McLaws' dispositions and ultimately decided they were too strong for him to attack head on. Late that morning cheering was heard in the southern ranks. When Federal skirmishers shouted across inquiring what the cheering was about, they were told that Harper's Ferry had surrendered. Early that afternoon, McLaws' brigades commenced to withdraw from Franklin's front and march down Pleasant Valley.

Fortunately for Lee, McLaws had disregarded Lee's orders to withdraw into Virginia. Believing his best chance for survival lay in bluffing Franklin and allowing Jackson to secure the surrender of Harper's Ferry, he kept up his bold front until news of the surrender arrived, then withdrew his command. Franklin sent a half-hearted pursuit after McLaws, but it kept its distance and McLaws escaped unmolested.

Jackson opened the 15th with a thundering bombardment of the Union positions near Harper's Ferry. By 10 A.M., the garrison had expended their artillery ammunition and the post commander, Colonel Dixon Miles, felt further resistance was futile. Moments after raising the white flag Miles was mortally wounded by a Confederate battery that failed to observe the signal of surrender. 12,737 men, 47 guns, and ample stores of clothing, equipment and other valuable items were surrendered to Jackson in the largest capitulation of U. S. troops in the entire war.

The opportunity that the discovery of Special Orders No. 191 provided McClellan to destroy the southern army was fast slipping through his fingers. Instead of planning the destruction of the three divisions Lee held west of Antietam Creek, he anticipated the Confederates would withdraw during the night to the safety of Virginia. No provisions or plan of attack was prepared in the event the southern divisions were still there in the morning.

The morning of September 16th dawned with a heavy fog that hampered visibility. Nevertheless, it was apparent that Lee had not withdrawn during the night, but was still in position. Instead of using the fog to put his army in motion to attack Lee, McClellan hesitated and spent the morning studying the ground and Confederate dispositions. While precious minutes ticked away, Jackson and Walker were marching rapidly to join Lee. McLaws and Anderson followed some distance behind, and A. P. Hill's Division had been left at Harper's Ferry to administer the surrender of the Federal troops.

By early afternoon, Jackson and Walker reached the field raising Lee's force to six divisions, or perhaps 27,000 men of all arms. Lee deployed these troops in an arc like perimeter with each flank anchored by the Potomac River. If McClellan was going to attack, it would have to be a frontal assault.

Not until Jackson's forces were streaming onto the field did McClellan move. He ordered Hooker's 1st Corps to cross the Antietam at an upper ford and bridge and develop the left flank of the Confederate position. The Confederate left offered the most favorable terrain for maneuver and attack, and it was here McClellan planned to make his main effort on the 17th. But by sending Hooker, alone and unsupported, across the Antietam on the 16th, he telegraphed clearly to Lee where the blow would fall the next day and exposed Hooker to defeat in detail.

Hooker sensed his vulnerability and requested reinforcements. McClellan responded that they would be forthcoming and would fall under Hooker's orders when they arrived. Shortly before sunset, Hooker's advance encountered Hood's Division in the East Woods. A sharp action developed that eventually subsided with most of the woods in Federal hands. A misty rain began to fall soaking the shivering men of both armies who lay on their arms in the inky darkness and awaited the dawn.

During the night, Major General Joseph K. Mansfield's 12th Corps was marched to the west bank of the Antietam and massed approximately one mile north of Hooker's 1st Corps. McClellan's plan for the 17th was to open his attack upon Lee's left with the 1st and 12th Corps, supported by Sumner and Franklin, who had been ordered to rejoin the army. Burnside would launch a diversionary attack upon Lee's left. When the attacks upon Lee's flanks were sufficiently developed, McClellan would advance his center and hopefully carry the day. In theory, it was an excellent plan. In implementation, it was abominably executed on McClellan's part and virtually assured there would be no cooperation between the various attacking corps.

Picket firing across Hooker's front continued throughout the night, and as dawn approached it intensified. Because his corps had reached its attack position so late in the day on the 16th, Hooker had not been able to thoroughly study the ground his corps would attack over. He planned to launch a rather unimaginative frontal assault using the Hagerstown Road as a guide for his advance. His corps' objective was the high ground around the white Dunker Church, which stood out sharply against the West Woods, crowding up against its rear. No provisions were made to assault Nicodemus Heights from which southern artillery could enfilade Hooker's entire advance, and which largely dominated much of Lee's left. This was no doubt the result of Hooker's ignorance of the ground.

Confronting Hooker were two divisions of Jackson's corps,

supported by Hood's Division and plentiful artillery. Between
5:30 A.M. and 6 A.M. Hooker's advance struck this line and
the Battle of Antietam had commenced.

Hooker's attack demolished Jackson's two divisions in nearly
an hour and one-half of bloody fighting. Jackson called upon
Hood and D. H. Hill, whose division occupied Lee's left
center, for support. Hood counterattacked violently and
hurled Hooker's advance back, but he in turn was
counterattacked by Hooker's reserve division and the battle
swayed back across farmer Miller's cornfield. Ripley and
Garland's brigades of Hill's Division arrived at this moment
and drove the Federals back across the cornfield, also
seizing a portion of the East Woods.

It was nearly 7 A.M. and Hooker had lost most of the 2,590
casualties his corps would suffer in the battle. Confederate
losses were equally severe. As Hooker's battered brigades
drifted back from the bloody conflict, they encountered
Mansfield's 12th Corps moving up to their support. Minutes
after his corps became engaged, Mansfield was mortally
wounded and command devolved upon Brigadier General Alpheus
Williams. Hooker, too, was wounded around this time, and
command of his corps fell to Brigadier General George Meade.
Williams pushed his corps into the fight, clearing the East
Woods of Confederate troops and crushing Colquitt's Brigade,
which had relieved Ripley.

By 9 A.M. the East Woods and cornfield were in Federal
hands, and the battle seemed to be progressing well for
McClellan. After some delay, he had started Sumner's 2d Corps
for the front, and at around 9 A.M., Sumner arrived upon the
scene with Sedgwick's Division. Without bothering to study
the situation Sumner plunged ahead into the West Woods with
Sedgwick's doomed command deployed in three parallel lines.

A mere handful of Confederates were initially available to
confront Sedgwick's advance. Twelve brigades had been chewed
up in the bloody conflict that had raged over the cornfield
and through the East Woods, and only Early's Brigade and
remnants of units stood in the way. However, reinforcements
were rushing to the rescue. Mclaws and Anderson's Divisions
had arrived at Sharpsburg early that morning after a grueling
night march. The divisions had halted west of Sharpsburg and
the men permitted to snatch some rest. When the desperate cry
for reinforcements arose from his beleagured left, Lee called
upon McLaws to march immediately to its support. As McClellan
had thus far remained inactive upon the other sectors of the
battlefield, Lee also pulled Walker's Division out of the
line on his far right and sent it hustling off to the left.

McLaws counterattack struck Sedgwick's Division squarely
upon its left flank. Because of its poor deployment the
division was unable to shift its strength to meet the attack
and in perhaps no more than 15 minutes Sedgwick lost 2,200
men and his division was completely routed. The Southern
attack boiled out of the West Woods, but the massed Union
artillery and 12th Corps infantry drove them back with heavy
losses. Greene's Division of the 12th Corps followed up this
success and gained a lodgement in the West Woods around the
Dunker Church. Despite his efforts to get reinforcements he

was unsuccessful, and a Confederate counterattack drove his division out of the woods around noon.

As the action on the Confederate left subsided the battle shifted to the Confederate center, where D. H. Hill's Division was posted defending the Sunken Lane.

General French's division of the 2d Corps, in its movement across Antietam Creek, became seperated from Sedgwick's division. When it reached the East Woods at around 9:30 A. M., French observed Greene's division laying down to his left front. French inclined his division to the left of Greene and soon bumped into Hill's well posted defenders. A furious battle quickly developed and French's losses mounted steadily. Unable to make headway against the terrific fire Hill's veterans were laying down, French's men simply halted, lay down and returned the fire.

Shortly after 10:30 A.M., Richardson's division of the 2d Corps arrived upon the field and began to add its weight to the battle. Across the musketry swept space Hill too was being reinforced. Anderson's Division was moved from its reserve position to bolster Hill's hard pressed line. Ultimately, Hill's line collapsed, and Richardson and French's battered brigades overran the Sunken Lane. The Confederate center was broken and defeat seemed likely. Remnants of the Confederate defenders were rallied around the Piper Farm, but the southern line was desperately thin. "It was easy to see that if the Federals broke through our line there, the Confederate army would be cut in two and probably destroyed, for we were already badly whipped and were only holding our ground by sheer force of desperation." recorded General Longstreet.

To throw the Federals off balance and conceal their weakness, Hill and Longstreet launched local counterattacks at various points. These were all beaten off, but the federals, exhausted and racked by heavy losses, grew wary and failed to press their advantage. General Richardson, an agressive soldier, might have mounted a renewed attack, but he was mortally wounded by a shell fragment. The fighting gradually subsided and a splendid opportunity to deal a crippling blow to Lee was lost.

During the furious fighting for the Sunken Lane, Franklin's 6th Corps arrived upon the field. Instead of directing it toward the center, to reinforce Richardson and French, McClellan dispatched it to his right, where a shaken General Sumner signaled that affairs were in a desperate state. Actual conditions were not so serious for the Confederates in the West Woods were not nearly strong enough to attack McClellan's right. But so agressive had the Confederate defense been throughout the day, Federal leaders were deceived as to the true strength of the southern army.

When Franklin reached the vicinity of the East Woods he immediately began to make preparations to assault the West Woods, but Sumner forbade it on the grounds that Franklin's two divisions represented the only reliable troops he had to resist a Confederate attack. McClellan soon appeared upon the scene, having crossed the Antietam to investigate the situation on his right personally. It was obvious that Sumner was badly shaken and possibly in no condition to make decisions, but McClellan refused to overule his judgement and Franklin's attack was cancelled.

Following Sedgwick's debacle and Sumner's urgent appeal for help, McClellan had ordered Burnside to move his 9th Corps forward and press Lee's right. To cross his artillery to the west bank of the Antietam it was necessary for Burnside to seize the stone bridge that carried the Rohrbach Road over the creek into Sharpsburg. Burnside had dispatched Rodman's Division to march down the creek, cross at Snavely's Ford, and outflank the bridge's defenders so as to avoid a costly frontal attack. But Rodman took longer than anticipated and McClellan sent repeated urgent orders directing Burnside to carry the bridge. Three unsuccessful attempts were made and not until noon did the bridge fall.

Burnside pushed his divisions across the Antietam throughout the early afternoon, and by 3 P.M. he was ready to commence a general advance by his entire corps. The attack jumped off and gained ground steadily. D.R. Jones' Division, which held Lee's right, was unable to contain the heavier number of Federals, and several of its brigades were driven from the field in confusion. Once again, victory seemed within McClellan's grasp. But just as success seemed to smile on Burnside's efforts, A. P. Hill's Division, which had made a 17 mile forced march from Harper's Ferry, suddenly appeared upon his left flank and launched an aggressive counterattack. The 9th Corps reeled back in retreat giving up its dearly bought gains. Hills' attack was stopped near sunset, but not before he had driven the Federals to the bluffs above Antieam Creek. The bloodiest single day in the American Civil War was over. Union losses totalled 2,108 dead, 9,549 wounded and 753 missing. The incomplete Confederate losses tallied around 12,000 dead, wounded and missing. Nearly 25,000 men had become battle casualties.

The following day, September 18th, Lee maintained his position. During the night he had been reinforced by thousands of stragglers pushed up from the army's depot at Winchester, so that his strength was about what it had been on the 17th. McClellan had also been reinforced substantially, but he declined to renew the battle.

Lee saw little to be gained by remaining north of the Potomac, and during the night of the 18th he withdrew to Virginia. McClellan started a half-hearted pursuit on the 19th. On the 20th, elements of the 5th Corps crossed the river near Sheperdstown. Lee smashed this bridgehead with a violent counterattack by A. P. Hill's Division. The federals sullenly withdrew and the Maryland Campaign came to a close.

What had been gained? What had been lost? Lee had indeed fought a magnificent battle at Antietam, outgeneraling McClellan at every turn. But aside from the capture of Harper's Ferry and its stores, his foray into Maryland had been a costly failure in manpower. McClellan had conducted his campaign and battle poorly, throwing away repeated opportunities to destroy Lee's army. Yet, in the end, Lee had been compelled to withdraw from Maryland and this was what proved to be significant.

Lincoln grasped the opportunity this withdrawal presented and released his Emancipation Proclamation, a document that completely altered the war. No longer would it be a war solely to restore the Union. Antietam had changed all that. It would now also be a war to abolish slavery. England and France, who had already abolished that institution, would now hesitate to lend their support to the Confederacy, dealing a blow to the South's hope for a European negotiated settlement. After Antietam the South could only hope for a military victory to gain their independence. This hope would perish on the bloodstained fields of Gettysburg.

2.
Manuscripts

NATIONAL ARCHIVES

1   Antietam Battlefield Board Papers, Record Group 92, Series
    707.
      Chiefly on the establishment and early administration of
    Antietam National Battlefield.

2   Antietam Studies. Record Group 94.
      Hundreds of letters from veterans to members of the
    Antietam Battlefield Commission concerning their
    experiences in the Battle of Antietam.

3   Army of the Potomac Papers.
      Official correspondence. Significant items were
    published in Official Records.

4   Headquarters of the Army of the Potomac. Record Group 108.
      Not much of importance that was overlooked in Official
    Records.

DARTMOUTH COLLEGE

5   John M. Gould Papers - Antietam Collection
      Massive correspondence from the late 1800's from Union
    and Confederate veterans who fought over the East Woods,
    Cornfield, and West Woods.

DUKE UNIVERSITY

6   John M. Gould Collection
      Contains Gould's wartime memoranda book, a wartime letter
    on Mansfield's death, and some Antietam related letters
    from members of the 10th Maine.

7   Lafayette McLaws Papers
      Some correspondence. Majority of McLaws papers are

located in Southern Historical Collection.

LIBRARY OF CONGRESS - MANUSCRIPT DIVISION

8   Ezra A. Carman Papers. "History of the Antietam
    Campaign."
    Carman was the Colonel of the 13th New Jersey at
    Antietam. He later served on Antietam Commission. This
    unpublished manuscript of over 1,200 pages describes the
    campaign in great detail.

9   Henry Hunt Papers.
     Contains official correspondence, battle reports from
    battery commanders, some personal correspondence of
    Hunt's, and strength figures for artillery in Maryland
    Campaign.

10 Jedediah Hotchkiss Papers.
    Hotchkiss was a cartographer on Jackson's staff. His
    papers include his extremely informative diary.

11 Marsena Patrick Journal.
    Patrick's journal was published in 1964 by David Sparks.

12 George B. McClellan Papers.
    Much important military correspondence from Maryland
    Campaign that was not published in the Official Records.

NEW YORK HISTORICAL SOCIETY

13 Ezra A. Carman Papers.
    Many pieces of correspondence with veterans. Also,
    Carman's notes concerning Maryland Campaign.

SOUTHERN HISTORICAL COLLECTION, UNIVERSITY OF NORTH CAROLINA

14 Edward Porter Alexander Papers.
    Correspondence with other southern officers concerning
    Maryland Campaign and Alexander's unpublished journal.

15 Daniel Harvey Hill Papers.
    Contains some correspondence between Hill and other
    notable Confederate officers relating to the Maryland
    Campaign.
    There are also Hill papers at the North Carolina State
    Archives and Virginia Historical Society.

16 James Longstreet Papers.
    Some correspondence with other Confederate officers
    relating to the Maryland Campaign. Many of the same
    correspondents as Hill. There is also a small collection
    of Longstreet post-war letters at Duke University.

17 Lafayette McLaws Papers.
    A large collection of official correspondence, personal

papers, wartime correspondence and post-war
correspondence.

VIRGINIA HISTORICAL SOCIETY

18 Robert E. Lee Headquarters Collection.
Official correspondence produced and received by army
headquarters. Significant correspondence was published in
the Official Records.

19 James E. B. Stuart Papers.
Some private correspondence and battle reports.

3.
Reference Works

20   Arnold, Louise. _The Era of the Civil War_. Carlisle
Barracks, PA: U.S. Army Military History Institute,
1982.
        A guide to one of the largest collections of Civil War
literature in the country.

21   Beers, Henry Putney. _Guide to the Archives of the
Government of the Confederate States of America_.
Washington, D.C.: Government Printing Office, 1968.
        An invaluable guide to researching any facet of the
Confederate States of America.

22   Boatner, Mark Mayo. _The Civil War Dictionary_. New York:
David McKay Co., 1959.

23   Dornbusch, C. E., comp. _Military Bibliography of the
Civil War_. 3 Vols.
        Vol. I. _Regimental Publications and Personal
Narratives of the Civil War: Northern States_. New
York: New York Public Library, 1962.
        Vol. II. _Regimental Publications and Personal
Narratives: Southern Border, and Western States and
Territories, Federal Troops_. New York: New York Public
Library, 1967.
        Vol. III. _General References, Armed Forces, and
Campaigns and Battles_. New York: New York Public Library,
1972.
        Vol. IV. _Regimental Publications and Personal
Narratives, Union and Confederate Biographies_. Dayton,
OH: Morningside Press, 1987.
        The most outstanding Civil War bibliography available.
Literally every regimental and personal narrative ever
published is listed.

24   Dyer, Frederick H. _A Compendium of the War of the
Rebellion Compiled and Arranged from Official Records
of the Federal and Confederate Armies_. Des Moines, IA:
Dyer, 1908.
        A wealth of information about both armies. Particularly

good for tracking down service records of individual
units.

25   Fox, William F. Regimental Losses in the American Civil
War, 1861-1865. Albany, N.Y.: Joseph McDonough, 1898.
      Lists the 300 "fighting regiments" of the Union army that
lost the greatest number of killed in battle. Full of
useful facts.

26   Livermore, Thomas L. Numbers and Losses in the Civil War
in America, 1861-1865. New York: Houghton, Mifflin,
1901.
      Livermore's estimates on numbers engaged and casualties
in every major battle of the war. Use with some caution.

27   Munden, Kenneth White, and Beers, Henry Putney. Guide
to Federal Archives Relating to the Civil War.
Washington, D.C.: Government Printing Office, 1962.
      A companion volume to the guide to Confederate archives.

28   Nevins, Allan; Robertson, James I., Jr.; Wiley, Bell I.,
eds. Civil War Books: A Critical Bibliography. 2 vols.
Baton Rouge: Louisiana State University Press, 1967.
      A reference guide to some 5,700 of the war's most
significant publications by three distinquished
historians.

29   Phisterer, Frederick. Statistical Record of the Armies
of the United States. New York: Charles Scribners Sons,
1883.
      A wealth of statistical information about the Union army.

30   Sellers, John R. Civil War Manuscripts. Washington,
D.C.: Government Printing Office, 1986.
      An annotated guide to the vast Civil War manuscript
holdings of the Library of Congress.

31   Sommers, Richard J. Manuscript Holdings of the Military
History Research Collection. 2 vols. Carlisle Barracks:
US Army Military History Research Collection, 1972-1975.
      Although this guide barely scratches the suface of
the 3,000+ manuscripts this facility holds, it is an
excellent starting point.

32   U. S. Department of the Army. Army Library. The Civil
War; A Catalog of Books in the Army Library Pertinent to
the American Civil War. Washington, D.C.: Department of
the Army, 1965.

33   U.S. National Archives. Guide to Cartographic Records
in the National Archives. Washington, D.C.: Government
Printing Office, 1971.
      Besides the Library of Congress map division, this is
the single most significant collection of Civil War maps.
Contains many with reference to Maryland Campaign.

34   U. S. National Archives and Records Service. General
Services Administration. A Military Operations of the
Civil War: Guide-Index to the Official Records of the
Union and Confederate Armies, 1861-1865. Washington, D.C.:
Government Printing Office, 1980.

35   U. S. War Department. The War of the Rebellion: A
Compilation of the Official Records of the Union and
Confederate Armies. 130 vols. Washington, D.C.: Government
Printing Office, 1880-1901.
      Volumes 19, in two parts, concerns the Maryland
Campaign. Volume 51, part one and two, contains much
correspondence on the campaign. Also see Volume 11 and 12.

36   _____. The Official Military Atlas of
the Civil War. New York: Arno Press, Crown Publishers,
1978.
      Reprint of 1891 edition. The most significant maps used
and produced during, and shortly after, the war. Several
valuable ones concerning Maryland Campaign included.

37   _____. Bibliography of State
Participation in the Civil War. Washington, D.C.
Government Printing Office, 1913.
      Many obscure titles although they can all be found in
Dornbusch.

4.
Campaign and Battle Histories

38   Allan, William. The Army of Northern Virginia in
1862. Boston and New York: Houghton and Mifflin, 1892.
        A useful, well balanced, objective account of the
campaign by a former ordnance officer under Jackson.

39   Anderson, John Henry. Notes on the Battles of
Fredricksburg and Antietam. London: H. Rees, 1912.

40   Cobb, Clarence F. McClellan's Antietam Campaign, 1862.
Washington, D. C.: Judd & Detweiter, 1891.
        An address delivered before the Maryland Historical
Society.

41   Frassanito, William Allan. Antietam, The Photographic
Legacy of America's Bloodiest Day. New York: Charles
Scribner's Sons, 1978.
        A study of the Gardner & Gibson photographs of the
battlefield. Outstanding work.

42   Freeman, Douglas S. Lee's Lieutenants, A Study in
Command, Vol. 2. New York: C. Scribner's Sons, 1946.
        Contains a general overview of Antietam with an
emphasis on southern leadership. Immensely readable,
superbly documented; somewhat opinionated.

43   Hess, George. Battlefield Guide of the Battles of
South Mountain and Antietam, Md., September 14-20, 1862.
Hagerstown, Md.: Globe Job Rooms Print, 1890.
        One of the early guides to Antietam.

44   ____,_____. The Maryland Campaign From September 1st
to September 20th, 1862. Hagerstown: Globe Job Rooms
Print, 1890.
        A brief outline of the campaign and battles.

45   Heysinger, Isaac Winter.Antietam and the Maryland and
Virginia Campaigns of 1862. New York: Neale Publishing,
1912.
        Very limited value. Undocumented, opinionated, and
unreasonably pro-McClellan.

46   Luvaas, Jay, and Nelson, Harold W., ed., The U. S.
Army War College Guide to the Battle of Antietam: The
Maryland Campaign of 1862. Carlisle, PA: South Mountain
Press, Inc., 1987.
        A thorough guide through the Maryland Campaign from
South Mountain to Harper's Ferry and Antietam.
Principally based upon officers' official reports.

47   McClellan, George B. The Complete Report on the
Organization and Campaigns of the Army of the Potomac.
n.p. 1864.
        Highly useful. Defensive in tone and employs
hindsight, but contains important campaign
correspondence.

48   Murfin, James V. The Gleam of Bayonets; The Battle of
Antietam and the Maryland Campaign of 1862. New York: T.
Yoseloff, 1965.
        Adequate documentation and generally well written
account of the battle and campaign. Hardcover edition
contains excellent tactical maps. Strongly pro-
Confederate and anti-McClellan.

49   Priest, John. Antietam: A Soldiers' Battle.
Shippensburg: White Mane Press, 1989.
        A soldiers' eye view of the battle. Contains over 70
tactical maps.

50   Reilly, O. T. The Battlefield of Antietam. Sharpsburg,
MD: Oliver T. Reilly, 1906.
        A guidebook for the battlefield. Some interesting
early 1900 photographs.

51   Schildt, John William. Drums Along the Antietam.
Parsons, West Virginia: McClain Print, 1972.
        Rich in details of local Sharpsburg history.

52   _____,_____. Four Days in October. n.p.,
1978.
        Concerns Lincoln's visit to the Army of the Potomac
after Antietam.

53   _____,_____. September Echoes; The Maryland
Campaign of 1862; The Places, the Battles, the Results.
Middletown, MD: Valley Register, 1960.
        Not a serious study of the campaign. Emphasis on human
interest stories.

54   Sears, Stephen W. Landscape Turned Red; The Battle of
Antietam. New Haven and New York: Ticknor & Field, 1983.
        Probably the most well-written, published account of
the Maryland Campaign. Fine appraisal of Lee and
McClellan's styles of command.

55   Sheppard, Eric W. The Campaign in Virginia and
Maryland, June 26th to Sept. 20th, 1862, Cedar Mountain,
Manassas, and Sharpsburg. London: G. Allen & co., 1911.
        A well written useful narrative. Written principally
for pre-World War I British officers.

56   Stackpole, Edward J. From Cedar Mountain to Antietam.
Harrisburg: Stackpole Co., 1959.
        Interesting interpretations but shallow research and
lack of documentation make it of limited value.

57   Tilbery, Frederick. Antietam National Battlefield
Site, Maryland. Washington: National Park Service, 1960.
        A fine encapsulated history of the Maryland Campaign
and Battle of Antietam, by a distinguished historian.

5.
Magazines and Newspapers

58   Alderman, Ira K. "The Ninth Corps at Antietam,"
National Tribune, February 20, 1908.
      Author served in 36th Ohio. Some personal incidents
recalled. Principally a defense of 9th Corps.

59   Allan, William. "Confederate Artillery at 2d Manassas
and Sharpsburg," _SHSP_, vol. 11 (1883), pp. 289-291.
      Artillery organization at above battles.

60   _____. "First Maryland Campaign," _SHSP_, vol.
14 (1886), pp. 102-118.
      A well balanced account of the campaign.

61   _____. "The Invasion of Maryland," _Southern
Bivouac_, Vol. II, no. 5 (Oct. 1886), pp. 300-306.
      Allan refutes various points made by James
Longstreet in a Century Magazine article.

62   Allen, George A. "After Antietam," _National Tribune_,
March, 1892.

63   Andrews, W. H. "Tige Anderson's Brigade at
Sharpsburg," _Confederate Veteran_, Vol. XVI (1908),
pp.578-580.
      Many personal details of Andrews service with G. T.
Anderson's Brigade at Sharpsburg.

64   Balsley, J. "Lee's Lost Order," _National Tribune_,
March 26, 1908.
      Balsley was a Captain in the 27th Indiana. Describes
in detail how order was discovered.

65   Barger, W. D. "Union and Confederate Monuments at
Sharpsburg," _Confederate Veteran_, Vol. XIX (1911), p.
495.
      For the 1911 tourist to Sharpsburg.

66   Barnes, Edward L. "The 95th New York: Sketch of its
Services in the Campaigns of 1862," National Tribune,
January 7, 1886.
        Describes South Mountain in good detail.

67   Bartlett, Joseph J. "Crampton's Pass," National
Tribune, December 19, 1889.
        The fullest and most detailed account of the forcing
of Crampton's Pass.

68   Beall, T. D. "Reminiscences About Sharpsburg,"
Confederate Veteran, Vol. I (1892), p. 246.
        Served with G. B. Anderson's Brigade. Concerns
infantry serving an abandoned gun after Sunken Lane had
fallen.

69   Beech, ?. "4th New Jersey at Crampton's Gap," National
Tribune, May 8, 1884.
        Fine account of Crampton's Gap.

70   Belknap, C. W. "Harper's Ferry," National Tribune,
July 26, 1894.
        Adds nothing new. Member of the 125th New York.

71   Bell, Thomas. "Capture of Longstreet's Ammunition
Train," National Tribune, July 3, 1894.
        Describes escape of cavalry from Harper's Ferry and
capture of part of Longstreet's reserve ordnance train.

72   Benning, Henry Lewis. "Notes on the Battle of
Sharpsburg," SHSP, vol. 16 (1888), pp. 393-395.
        Concerns defense of "Burnside's Bridge," by Toombs
Georgians.

73   Blausum, Daniel F. "Personal Reminiscences of Sergeant
Daniel F. Blausum, Co. K, 48th Regiment, Pennsylvania
Volunteer Infantry," Publications of the Historical
Society of Schuykill County, Vol. IV (1914), pp. 240-249.

74   Bond, Frank A. "General Lee Trusting in Providence at
Antietam," Century Magazine, November, 1886 to April,
1887, p. 309.
        Concerns incident on Confederate left.

75   Bradley, C. E. "On Antietam Field," National Tribune,
September 10, 1896.
        By a member of the 32nd North Carolina. Describes
postwar visit.

76   Bradwell, I. G. "General Lee at Sharpsburg,"
Confederate Veteran, Vol. XXIX (1921), pp. 378-380.
        Principally describes action Douglass' Georgia Brigade
participated in. Author served in 31st Georgia.

77   Breen, Patrick. "Why the Union Army Did Not Win at
Antietam," National Tribune, April 18, 1895.
        Breen served with the 2d U.S. Infantry.

78   Bresnahan, John. "Battle of Antietam," National
Tribune, February 21, 1889.
        Fighting in Miller's Cornfield by a member of the 27th
Indiana.

79   Brown, Kent Masterson. "Battle for the Dunkard
Church," Virginia Country's Civil War Quarterly, Vol. IX,
(1987) pp. 35-45.
        A basic narrative of operations around the Dunkard
Church.

80   Buch, Jacob. "Gen. Mansfield's Death," National
Tribune, April 13, 1893.
        Somewhat unusual account of 12th Corps commander,
Joseph K. Mansfield's, death, by a courier attached to
12th Corps headquarters.

81   Burnham, Uberto A. "South Mountain," National Tribune,
May 24, 1928.
        Describes battle in general terms, but also contains
many details of his regiment's (76th New York)
participation.

82   Campbell, Gabriel. "Charge of the Stonewall Regiment,"
Dartmouth Magazine, XVII (1903), pp. 241-244.
        The 17th Michigan at South Mountain.

83   Casey, James B., ed., "The Ordeal of Adoniram Judson
Warner: His Minutes of South Mountain and Antietam,"
Civil War History, Vol. XXVIII, no. 3 (September, 1982),
pp. 213-236.
        A full, minutely detailed narrative of Warner's
experiences as the commander of the 10th Pennsylvania
Reserves.

84   Castel, Albert. "George B. McClellan: Little Mac,"
CWTI, Vol. XIII, no. 2 (May, 1974), pp. 4-11.
        A good objective article. Gives McClellan credit where
credit is due.

85   Castor, L. F. "Soldier Writes of the Battle of
Antietam," National Tribune, April 24, 1930.
        A letter Castor wrote on Sept. 28, 1862 describing
battle. He served with 28th Pennsylvania.

86   Chisholm, Alexander R. "The Battle of Antietam," SHSP,
Vol. 31 (1903), pp. 43-45.
        Principally concerns strengths of armies at
Sharpsburg.

87   Conline, John. "Recollections of the Battle of
Antietam and the Maryland Campaign," War Papers, Vol. II,
pp. 110-116. (Commandery of the State of Michigan,
MOLLUS.) Detroit: James H. Stone and Co., 1898.
        Conline served with the 4th Vermont. Contains some
information about the Vermont Brigade at Crampton's Gap.

88   Copehart, Henry. "Replies to Criticism on Stonewall
Jackson at Antietam," National Tribune, August 4, 1892.

89   Cornett, J. L. "The Battle of Antietam," PWP, April
21, 1886.
        Concerns Tyndale's Brigade.

90   Corning, Joseph L. "The 28th Pennsylvania at
Antietam," Grand Army Scout and Soldiers Mail, Vol. II
(September 22, 1883).
        Highly detailed account of the 28th at Antietam.

91   Cummings, C. C. "Mississippi Boys at Sharpsburg,"
Confederate Veteran, Vol. V, pp. 23-24.
        Human interest story of the 17th Mississippi.

92   _____. "Sharpsburg - Antietam," Confederate
Veteran, Vol. XXIII (1915), p. 199.
        Cummings personal observations and experiences in the
battle.

93   _____. "Storming Maryland Heights,"
Confederate Veteran, Vol. XXIII (1915), p. 124.
        Experiences of Barksdale's Brigade in battle for
Maryland Heights.

94   Cutts, A. S. "Cutts' Battalion at Sharpsburg," SHSP,
vol. 10 (1882), pp.430-431.
        Letter to J. W. Jones, August 24, 1882 concerning
composition of battalion and its operations.

95   Davis, George Breckenridge. "The Antietam Campaign,"
Papers of the Military Historical Society of
Massachusetts, Vol. III, pp. 27-72. (Commandery of the
State of Massachusetts, MOLLUS.) Boston, n.d.
        Davis served with the 1st Maine Cavalry. He served as
a commissioner at Antietam in the late 1800's.

96   Dawes, Rufus R. "On the Right at Antietam," Sketches
of War History, Vol. III, pp. 252-263. (Commandery of the
State of Wisconsin, MOLLUS.) Cincinnati: Robert Clarke
and Co., 1888.
        Dawes' outstanding account of fighting in Miller's
Cornfield with the 6th Wisconsin.

97   Daniel, John Warwick. "One of the Gamest of Modern
Fights," SHSP, vol. 33 (1905), pp. 97-99.
        Concerns Col. E. M. Morrison and the 15th Virginia
Infantry at Sharpsburg.

98   DeRosset, William L. "Ripley's Brigade at Antietam,"
Century Magazine, November 1886 to April 1887, p. 309.
        An officer of the 3rd North Carolina explains why
Ripley's Brigade was not engaged at South Mountain.

99   Dixon, William D. "From Antietam to Fredricksburg,"
PWP, June 15, 1887.

100   Dodson, R. T. "With Stuart in Maryland in 1862," PWP,
March 8, 1884.
        Services in the horse artillery.

101   _____, ____. "Sharpsburg," PWP, October 24, 1885.
        A Confederate horse artilleryman's recollections.

102   Doubleday, Abner. "Letter From Major General Abner
Doubleday on Detail of the Battle of Antietam," National
Tribune, March 24, 1892.

103   Douglas, Henry K. "The Battle of Antietam," PWP, April
8, 1882.
        A staff officer of Jackson's account of the battle.

104   Dunnigan, Edward R. "Mansfield's Wounding," National
Tribune, July 7, 1892.
        Concerns the dispute over where 12th Corps commander,
Joseph K. Mansfield was mortally wounded.

105   Dwyer, John. "Crampton's Pass," National Tribune, May
5, 1892.
        Has nothing to do with Battle of Crampton's Pass.
Rather, about passing over Turner's Pass. Served in 63rd
New York.

106   Dye, John H. "Was Miles a Traitor," National Tribune,
October 22, 1891.
        The debate over Dixon Miles by a member of the 115th
New York.

107   Elble, Sigmund. "General Dixon Miles," National
Tribune, March 3, 1892.
        Elble served with the 3rd U. S. infantry.

108   Evans, Thomas H. "An Eyewitness Account of Antietam,"
CWTI, Vol. VII, no. 1 (April, 1968), pp. 32-40.
        A Lieutenant in the 12th U. S. Regulars observant
recollections of service at Antietam.

109   Faulk, Phil F. "Hartstuff's Brigade," National
Tribune, September 1, 1892.
        Personal reminiscences by a member of the 11th
Pennsylvania.

110   _____,_____. "South Mountain," PWP, August 12, 1882.
        Experiences of Hartstuff's Brigade at South Mountain.

111   Fishel, Edwin C. "Pinkerton and McClellan: Who
Deceived Whom?" Civil War History, Vol. XXXIV, no. 2
(June, 1988), pp. 115-142.
        Although it does not concern Antietam, the article is
illuminating about McClellan and his enemy strength
figures.

112   Fisher, Edward. "Battle of Antietam," National
Tribune, January 3, 1907.
        Fisher served with 130th Pennsylvania. Many details
and personal observations of battle.

113   Fortin, Maurice S., ed., "Colonel Hilary A. Herbert's
History of the Eight Alabama Volunteer Regiment, C.S.A,"
Alabama Historical Quarterly, Vol. XXXIX (1977), pp. 5-
321.
        The first 196pp deal with the regiment's history and
contain some description of Antietam. The rest is a
roster.

114   Fout, Fred W. "Miles at Harper's Ferry," National
Tribune, September 19, 1901.
        Detailed, but questionable account of Dixon Miles.
Author served with 15th Indiana Battery.

115   Frassanito, William A. "The Photographers of
Antietam," CWTI, Vol. XVII, no. 5 (August, 1978).
        Written by the authority on Civil War photographers.

116   Frye, Dennis E. "The Siege of Harper's Ferry," Blue
and Gray, Vol. V, no. 1 (1987).
        A fine study of this overlooked aspect of the Maryland
Campaign, by the historian of Harper's Ferry NHP.

117   Gallagher, Gary. "The Confederate Defense of the
Sunken Road at Sharpsburg," Virginia Country's Civil War
Quarterly, Vol. IX (1987), pp. 57-64.
        A good, short description of this phase of the battle.

118   Garnett, James Mercer. "The Battle of Antietam," SHSP,
vol. 31 (1891), pp. 32-37.
        Operations of J. R. Jones Division by a staff officer
in the Stonewall Brigade.

119   Gerrish, Theodore. "The Field of Antietam," National
Tribune, October 5, 1882.
        Gerrish served with the 20th Maine.

120   Goldsborough, C. E. "Blue and Butternut," National
Tribune, October 14, 1886.
        Fascinating account of the Confederate occupation of
Frederick, Maryland.

121   Goodheart, Briscoe. "Not Justifiable," National
Tribune, July 2, 1891.

One of many articles complaining that Miles commited a traitorous act by surrendering Harper's Ferry.

122   Gorman, George, ed., "Memoirs of a Rebel, Part I," Military Images, Vol. III, no. 3 (1981).
The military memoirs of Captain John C. Gorman of the 2d North Carolina. Vivid recollections of both South Mountain and Antietam.

123   Gould, John M. "Extract Gould's History of the 10th Maine," National Tribune, May 22, 1884.
The first time Gould raised the question of where Mansfield was mortally wounded.

124   _____,_____. "At Antietam." National Tribune, August 25, 1892.
Principally discusses the mortal wounding of Mansfield. Gould was the adjutant in the 10th Maine Infantry.

125   _____,_____. "Battle of Antietam," National Tribune, October 17, 1892.
Yet another on the Mansfield controversy.

126   _____,_____. "Antietam," National Tribune, March 23, 1893.
Gould continues Mansfield debate.

127   _____,_____. "Mansfield's Wounding," National Tribune, May 24, 31, 1906.
Gould tries to get the last word in on where Mansfield was mortally wounded.

128   Gratton, George D. "The Battle of Boonsboro Gap," SHSP, Vol 39 (1895), pp. 31-45.
Gratton was an aide to Colonel Alfred Colquitt. Although much of the account concerns official sources Gratton provides many personal observations.

129   Greene, A. Wilson. "Ambrose Burnside and the Ninth Corps at Antietam," Virginia Country's Civil War Quarterly, Vol. IX (1987), pp. 65-77.
A well written, perceptive article.

130   Groene, Bertram H., ed., "Civil War Letters of Colonel David Lang," Florida Historical Quarterly, Vol. LIV (1976), pp. 340-366.
Contains one letter Lang, Colonel of the 8th Florida, wrote from Frederick, Maryland, describing experiences and feelings.

131   Hall, Henry Seymour. "Experiences in the Peninsular and Antietam Campaigns," War Talks in Kansas, Vol. 1, pp. 160-161. (Commandery of the State of Kansas, MOLLUS.) Kansas City: Franklin Hudson Publishing House, 1906.
Hall's personal experiences with the 27th New York

Infantry.

132   ____, _____. "Personal Experiences Under
General McClellan, after Bull Run, Including the
Peninsula and Antietam Campaigns, from July 27, 1861, to
November 10, 1862," War Papers, (Commandery of the State
of Kansas, MOLLUS.) n.p., January 3, 1894.

133   Hamby, W. R. "Hood's Texas Brigade at Sharpsburg,"
Confederate Veteran, Vol. XVI (1908), pp. 19-20.
Describes action of entire brigade interspersed with
some personal details.

134   Hanger, J. E. "Echoes of the War; General Reno's
Death," National Tribune, August 23, 1883.
Describes circumstances surrounding Reno's death at
South Mountain.

135   Hargrove, J. G., ed., "General Bragg's Reminicences,"
Wisconsin Magazine of History, Vol. XXXIII (1950), pp.
281-309.
Recollections of Colonel (at Antietam) Edward Bragg of
the 6th Wisconsin Infantry.

136   Harries, William Henry. "In the Ranks at Antietam,"
Glimpses of the Nation's Struggle, Vol. IV, pp. 550-566.
(Commandery of the State of Minnisota, MOLLUS.) St. Paul,
St. Paul Book and Stationary Co., 1890.
Harries service with the 2nd Wisconsin at Antietam.
Lacks personal detail.

137   Hartranft, John F. "The Stone Brigade At Antietam,"
Grand Army Scout and Soldiers Mail, Vol. III (November
22, 1884).
Hartranft's 51st Pennsylvania was one of the two
regiments that forced "Burnside's Bridge." This is his
description of the fight.

138   Healy, W. H. "That Artillery at Sharpsburg,"
Confederate Veteran, Vol. III (1895), p. 131.
Served with Woofolk's Battery.

139   Henderson, Vernon F. "Diary of a Pennsylvania
Reserve," National Tribune, August 29, 1901.
Henderson's 1862 diary.

140   Heysinger, Isaac Winter. "The Cavalry Column From
Harper's Ferry," Journal of the United States Cavalry
Association, Vol. XXIV (1914), pp. 587-638.
A full account of the daring cavalry escape by a
member of the 7th Rhode Island Squadron.

141   Hicks, Josiah D. "Death of Gen. Mansfield," National
Tribune, December 27, 1917.
Hicks served with 125th Pennsylvania. Cites evidence
to support claim that Mansfield was shot near the 125th.

142   Higgins, Jacob. "At Antietam. The Gallant Services of
the 125th Pennsylvania," National Tribune, June 3, 1886.
     Highly detailed personal reminscences of the 125th's
service at Antietam, by their Colonel.

143   Hill, Daniel H. "The Lost Dispatch," SHSP, Vol. 13
(1885), pp. 420-423.
     Hill presents his arguments why he did not lose S. O.
191.

144   Hinkly, John. "Battle of Antietam," National Tribune,
July 7, 1892.
     Fine personal account by a member of the 3rd Wisconsin.

145   Hobart, Barth. "Battle of Antietam," National Tribune,
February 16, 1893.
     Hobart served with 125th Pennsylvania. Article
principally concerned with Mansfield's mortal wounding.

146   Hoffsommer, Robert D. Jackson's Capture of Harper's
Ferry," CWTI, Vol. I, no. 5 (August, 1962), pp. 12-13.
     A very brief description of the Confederate operation
against Harper's Ferry.

147   Holsinger, Frank. "The Dunker Church," National
Tribune, April 9, 1908.
     Describes appearence of Dunker Church during battle.

148   Hooker, Joseph. "Hooker on McClellan," National
Tribune, November 14, 1907.
     A letter from Hooker to Hon. J. W. Nesmith on July 7,
1862 describing his feelings about McClellan.

149   Howard, Oliver O. "General Howard's Personal
Reminiscences," National Tribune, March 6, 13, 20, 27,
April 10, 1884.
     Contains a well-balanced account of the entire
Maryland Campaign and Battle of Antietam.

150   Howard, William F. "Special Orders No. 191 and the
Maryland Campaign of 1862," Virginia Country Civil War
Quarterly, Vol. IX (1987), pp. 27-34.
     The loss of S. O. 191 and their impact upon the
campaign.

151   Hunter, Alexander. "The Battle of Sharpsburg," SHSP,
vol. 10, (1882) pp.503-512; vol. 31 (1903), pp. 37-43.
     Hunter served with the 17th Virginia. Excellent
account of life in the Confederate ranks in Maryland.

152   Hutchinson, A. H. "General Mansield's Death," National
Tribune, September, 1892.
     Hutchinson was a courier on Mansfield's staff.

153   Huyette, Miles C. "On a Bloody Field," National
Tribune, November 30, 1893.

Principally accounts from the Offical Records. Huyette
served in the 125th Pennsylvania.

154   Johnson, Bradley T. "First Maryland Campaign," SHSP,
vol. 12 (1884), pp. 500-537.
Some interesting details. Confederate viewpoint.

155   Johnston, David E. "McIntosh's Battery at Sharpsburg,"
Confederate Veteran, Vol. XIX (1911), p. 585, Vol. XX,
p. 204.
Johnston served in the 7th Virginia.

156   _____. "Concerning the Battle of
Sharpsburg," Confederate Veteran, Vol. VI (1896), p. 27.
Johnston served with 7th Virginia. Describes his
unit's experiences in the campaign and at Sharpsburg.

157   Johnston, James Steptoe. "A Reminiscence of
Sharpsburg," SHSP, vol. 8 (1880), pp. 526-529.
Served in 4th Alabama.

158   Jones, A. C. "Incidents of the Battle of Sharpsburg,"
Confederate Veteran, Vol. XV (1907), p. 507.
Incidents involving Manning's Brigade of Walker's
Division.

159   Kelly, Dennis. "The Battle of Shepardstown," CWTI,
Vol. XX, no. 7 (November, 1981), pp. 8-15.
One of the few items on a largely overlooked action.

160   Key, J. C. "Georgians and Tar Heels at Sharpsburg,"
Confederate Veteran, Vol. IX (1901), pp. 405-406.
Ripley's Brigade at Antietam.

161   Klesnfelter, H. G. "Battery B at Antietam," National
Tribune, May 8, 1890.
A letter to August Buell from Klesnfelter describing
his services with the 7th Wisconsin at Antietam.

162   Little, Henry. "Reno's Death; Another Account,"
National Tribune, August 2, 1883.
Many details. Little was a member of Reno's personal
escort.

163   Lounsberry, William. "The Ulster Regiment in the
"Great Rebellion," Collections of the Ulster Historical
Society, Vol. L (1860/1862), pp. 210-218.
Brief history of the 80th New York Infantry (20th New
York State Militia.)

164   Maury, Dabney Herndon. "McClellan and Lee at
Sharpsburg," SHSP, vol. 8 (1880), pp. 261-266.

165   McCormack, John F. Jr., "Harper's Ferry Skedaddlers,"
CWTI, Vol. XIV, no. 8 (December, 1975), pp. 32-39.
Another in a long line of articles on the escape of

the Union cavalry from Harper's Ferry.

166   McCormack, John F. Jr., "The Irish Brigade," <u>CWTI</u>,
Vol. VIII, no. 1, (April, 1969), pp. 36-44.
Fairly basic encapsulated unit history.

167   McCoy, T. F. "The 107th Pennsylvania at South
Mountain, Antietam, and Fredricksburg," <u>PWP</u>, January 4,
1888.

168   McLaws, Lafayette. "The Capture of Harper's Ferry,"
<u>PWP</u>, September 5, 12, 19, 1888.
A must for understanding the operations of McLaws
command.

169   Michell, Harry W. "The Fighting Fourteenth," <u>Brooklyn
Advance</u>, Vol. XI (1885), pp. 253-256, Vol XII (1885), pp.
116-120.
The 14th Brooklyn (84th New York Infantry) at South
Mountain and Antietam.

170   Mies, John W. "Breakout at Harper's Ferry," <u>Civil War
History</u>, Vol. II, no. 2 (June, 1956), pp. 13-28.
A good, although dramatic account of the cavalry
escape.

171   Mockbee, R. T. "Why Sharpsburg Was a Drawn Battle,"
<u>Confederate Veteran</u>, Vol. XVI (1908), p. 160.
Concerns effect of A. P. Hill's counterattack upon the
outcome of the battle.

172   Monroe, John Albert. "Battery D, First Rhode Island
Light Artillery at the Battle of Antietam, September 17,
1862," <u>Personal Narratives Rhode Island Soldiers and
Sailors Historical Society</u>, Series 3, no. 16. Providence:
The Society, 1886.
Vivid first hand account of the battle by Battery D's
commander.

173   _____,_____. "Reminiscences of the War of the
Rebellion of 1861-1865," <u>Personal Narratives Rhode Island
Soldiers and Sailors Historical Society</u>. Series 2, no.
11. Providence: The Society, 1881.
Monroe's wartime experiences including Antietam.

174   Moore, J. B. "Battle of Sharpsburg," <u>SHSP</u>, vol. 27
(1899), pp. 210-219.
Largely concerned with Shepardstown. Moore served in
artillery battalion of A. P. Hill's Division.

175   Morrison, Emmett M. "Fifteenth Virginia at
Sharpsburg," <u>SHSP</u>, vol. 33 (1905), pp. 99-110.
Highly detailed account of Semmes Brigade in action
against Sedgwick's Division.

176   Morrison, J. G. "Jackson at Harper's Ferry," PWP,
December 22, 1883.
        Morrison was on Jackson's staff.

177   Morse, Charles Fessenden. "From Second Bull Run to
Antietam," Papers and Personal Reminiscences 1861-1865,
Vol. I, pp. 268-277. (Commandery of the State of
Missouri, MOLLUS.) St. Louis: Becktold and Co., 1892.
        Morse's experiences with the 2nd Massachusetts
Infantry.

178   Murfin, James V. "Lee's Lost Orders," CWTI, Vol. I,
no. 5 (August, 1962), pp. 28-31.
        Standard account.

179   Naisawald, L. VanLoan. "Why Confederates Invaded
Maryland," CWTI, Vol. I, no. 5 (August, 1962), pp. 19-27.
        A competent, well written discussion of why Lee moved
north.

180   Napier, Dr. J. L. "McIntosh's Battery at Sharpsburg,"
Confederate Veteran, Vol. XIX (1911), p. 429.
        Concerns whether McIntosh's Battery was overrun or
not.

181   Nichols, William. "Harper's Ferry," National Tribune,
June 25, 1891.
        Member of Rhode Island Cavalry detachment describes
cavalry's escape from Harper's Ferry.

182   _____,_____. "The Siege and Capture of Harper's
Ferry, by the Confederates, September, 1862," Personal
Narratives Rhode Island Soldiers and Sailors Historical
Society, Series 4, no. 2. Providence: The Society, 1889.
        Nichols interpretation of the siege and capture.

183   _____,_____. "Was Miles a Traitor," National
Tribune, December 24, 1891.
        Nichols adds his voice to the debate.

184   Nye, Wilbur S. "Profiles of Key Commanders," CWTI,
Vol. I, no. 5 (August, 1962), pp. 32-37.
        Profiles of officers at Antietam.

185   O'Brien, Jean G. "Clara Barton Brought Mercy to
Antietam," CWTI, Vol. I, no. 5 (August, 1962), pp. 38-39.
        Clara Barton's significant contribution to the care of
the wounded after Antietam.

186   Otis, H. E. "Tracing the Lines," National Tribune, May
7, 1896.
        Served in 12th Ohio. Useful account.

187   Otis, J. E. "The Cannoneer," National Tribune, April
10, 1890.

Letter to Augustus Buell from Otis, a member of the 7th Wisconsin, describing his unit's participation.

188   Owen, Henry T. "South Mountain," PWP, July 31, 1880.
Perhaps the best Confederate account of South Mountain. Author was in 8th Virginia.

189   Palfrey, Francis. "The Battle of Antietam," Papers of the Military Historical Society of Massachusetts, Vol. III, pp. 1-26. (Commandery of the State of Massachusetts, MOLLUS.)
A shorter overview of the campaign and battle than Palrey's book The Antietam and Fredricksburg.

190   Parham, John T. "Thirty-Second at Sharpsburg," SHSP, vol. 34, pp. 250-253.
32nd Virginia. Parham describes some details of Crampton's Gap in addition to Antietam.

191   Potter, Wilbur A. "Antietam," National Tribune, September 2, 1886.
The 21st Massachusetts story of crossing Burnside's Bridge.

192   Powell, Eugene. "Recollections of the Eastern Campaigns of the Fall of 1862," National Tribune, June 20, 27, 1901.
Fine account of Greene's Division fighting in the East Woods by the Lieutenant Colonel of the 66th Ohio.

193   Putnam, J. R. "Patrick's Brigade," National Tribune, April 30, 1908.
Describes morning action in West Woods. Putnam served with the 23rd New York.

194   Richardson, C. A. "Account of the Battle of Sharpsburg," Confederate Veteran, Vol. XVI (1908), p. 20.
Principally facts and figures about the battle.

195   _____. "Sharpsburg Compared to Waterloo," Confederate Veteran, Vol. XIV (1906), p. 550.

196   _____. "General Lee at Sharpsburg," Confederate Veteran, Vol. XV (1907), pp. 411-412.
Richardson describes Lee's appearence during the battle through his personal observations.

197   _____. "Incidents of the Battle of Sharpsburg," Confederate Veteran, Vol. XV (1907), p. 380.
Richardson served with the 15th Virginia. Article concerns some of his personal experiences.

198   Robertson, James I., ed., "A Federal Surgeon At Sharpsburg," Civil War History, Vol. VI, no. 2 (June, 1960), pp. 134-151.
The excellent journal of Surgeon Theodore Dimon of the

2d Maryland Infantry. Many fascinating personal
observations.

199   Robbins, William M. "Battle of Antietam," National
Tribune, July 16, 1891.
        Concerns an incident that occured near the East Woods
on the night of September 16th. Robbins served in 4th
Alabama.

200   Round, A. S. "Antietam," National Tribune, July 1,
1886.
        Served in 34th New York. Describes action in West
Woods.

201   Sanderson, W. H. "Harper's Ferry and Its Surrender,"
National Tribune, September 28, 1893.
        Served in 9th Vermont.

202   _____,_____. "Harper's Ferry and Its Surrender,"
National Tribune, October 5, 1893.

203   Schell, Frank H. "A Great Raging Battlefield is Hell,"
CWTI, Vol. VIII (June, 1969) pp. 15-22.
        Illustrator Frank Schell describes his experiences at
Antietam.

204   Schenck, Martin. "Burnside's Bridge," Civil War
History, Vol. II, no. 4 (December, 1956), pp. 5-19.
        Poorly researched. Not reliable.

205   Searles, Jasper Newton. "The First Minnisota Volunteer
Infantry," Glimpses of the Nation's Struggle, II,
(Commandary of the State of Minnisota, MOLLUS.) St. Paul:
St. Paul Book and Stationary Company, 1890.
        Brief history of the 1st Minnisotat.

206   Sears, Stephen. "Landscape Turned Red," CWTI, Vol.
XXII, no. 4 (June, 1983), pp. 20-33.
        Excerpts from Sears book of the above name.

207   _____,_____. "America's Bloodiest Day: The Battle
of Antietam," CWTI, Vol. XXVI, no. 2 (April, 1987) pp. 2-
47.
        A special issue for CWTI on Antietam.

208   _____._____. "South Mountain," Blue and Gray, Vol.
IV, no. 1 (1986) pp. 3 - 62.
        Literally the only modern study of this neglected
battle.

209   _____._____. "Antietam," Blue and Gray, Vol. III,
no. 1 (1985).
        Differs somewhat in content from Sears article for
CWTI.

210   Shaw, Joseph. "Crampton's Pass," National Tribune,
        October 1, 1891.
        A fine personal account of battle by member of the
        95th Pennsylvania.

211   Shearer, Robert A. "Hartstuff's Brigade," National
        Tribune, September 15, 1892.
        Describes actions of his brigade and regiment (11th
        Pennsylvania).

212   Shepard, Henry E. "D. H. Hill at Sharpsburg,"
        Confederate Veteran, Vol. XXVI (1918), p. 72.
        Details of Hill's numerous courageous acts at
        Sharpsburg.

213   Smith, James O. "My First Campaign and Battles, A
        Jersey Boy at Antietam, Seventeen Days From Home," Blue
        and Gray, I (1893), pp. 280-290.
        Smith served in the 13th New Jersey.

214   Smith, Sol R. "South Mountain," National Tribune,
        January 17, 1895.
        The 12th Ohio at South Mountain.

215   Spooner, Henry Joshua. "The Maryland Campaign With the
        Fourth Rhode Island," Personal Narratives Rhode Island
        Soldiers and Sailors Historical Society, Series 6, no. 5.
        Providence, The Society, 1903.
        Spooner's personal experience with a rookie regiment
        in its first test of battle.

216   Squires, Charles W. " 'Boy Officer' of the Washington
        Artillery - Part I" CWTI, Vol. XIV, no. 2 (May, 1975),
        pp. 10-24.
        Squires memoirs of artillery service in Maryland with
        the Washington Artillery.

217   Stackpole, Edward J. "Showdown at Sharpsburg - Story
        of the Battle," CWTI, Vol. I, no. 5 (August, 1962), pp.
        6-11.
        Stackpole is a competent writer, but his research is
        rather sketchy.

218   Stickley, E. E. "Wounded at Sharpsburg," Confederate
        Veteran, Vol. XXV (1907), pp. 399-400.
        Author served in Stonewall Brigade. Many personal
        details including detailed description of his evacuation
        and treatment for wounds.

219   Stowe, Jonathan P. "Life With the 15th Mass.," CWTI,
        Vol. XI, no. 5 (August, 1972).
        Sgt. Stowe's diary. Contains a tragic entry as he lies
        mortally wounded in the West Woods.

220   Stuart, James T. "An Incident of the Battle of
Antietam," National Tribune, December 19, 1899.
        Human interest story concerning the burial of a
Captain of the 7th PA reserves during Antietam.

221   Taylor, Walter Herron. "The Battle of Sharpsburg,"
SHSP, vol. 24 (1896), pp. 267-274.
        Overview of battle with strength of Confederate army.

222   Thompson, Benjamin W. "This Hell of Destruction,"
CWTI, Vol. XII, no. 6 (October, 1973), pp. 12-23.
        Thompson's experiences with the 111th New York at
Harper's Ferry.

223   Thompson, David L. "In The Ranks to the Antietam,"
Battles and Leaders, vol. II, pp.556-558.
        Thompson's outstanding description of his personal
experiences with the 9th New York up to Antietam.

224   _____, _____. "With Burnside at Antietam,"
Battles and Leaders, Vol. II, pp.660-662.
        The conclusion of Thompson's experiences during the
Maryland Campaign.

225   Tillinghast, G. F. "Antietam Bridge," National
Tribune, December 30, 1886.
        Who crossed the bridge first, by a member of the 11th
Connecticut.

226   Venn, F. H. "That Flag of Truce at Antietam,"
Confederate Veteran, Vol. IV (1896), p. 389.
        Interesting incident that occured in vicinity of Piper
Farm and Sunken Lane on September 18th.

227   Vernon, George W. "Harper's Ferry," National Tribune,
March 30, 1893.
        Concerns cavalry escape from Harper's Ferry.

228   Walton, J. E. "Antietam," National Tribune, September
2, 1886.
        Concerns controversy of who crossed Burnside's Bridge
first.

229   Washburn, Charles E. "Was Miles a Traitor," National
Tribune, December 31, 1891.

230   Wert, Jeffery D. "The Battle of Sheperdstown,"
Virginia Country's Civil War Quarterly, Vol. IX (1987),
pp. 78-81.

231   ____, _____. "Lee and His Staff," CWTI, Vol. XI,
no. 4 (July, 1972), pp. 4-9.
        A useful article on the men who composed Lee's staff
and how he used them.

232   West, Robert. "Reno's Death," <u>National Tribune</u>, August 2, 1883.
        Detailed description by a member of the 51st New York.

233   Wilkins, A. C. "Antietam", <u>National Tribune</u>, January 9, 1908.
        Recollections of Maryland Campaigns with 4th Pennsylvania Cavalry.

234   Williams, H. David. "Johnny Reb and the Antietam Campaign," <u>Virginia Country's Civil War Quarterly</u>, Vol. IX (1987), pp. 13-26.
        The Confederate common soldier in the Maryland Campaign.

235   Williams, Horace N. "Rodman's Brigade at Antietam," <u>National Tribune</u>, December 9, 1886.
        Some interesting details on Williams service with 8th Connecticut.

236   Williams, John E. "General Miles Character," <u>National Tribune</u>, December 12, 1891.

237   Williams, John T. "Harper's Ferry," <u>National Tribune</u>, July 30, 1891.
        Served in the 32nd Ohio. Not worth consulting.

238   Williams, John T. "Was Miles a Traitor?" <u>National Tribune</u>, September 24, 1891.
        Williams perpetuates the myth that Dixon Miles was killed by his own artillery.

239   Wistar, Isaac J. "A Noted Charge at Antietam," <u>PWP</u>, February 18, 1882.
        Wistar was the Colonel of the 71st Penna.

240   Yard, William C. "Antietam," <u>National Tribune</u>, November 1, 1894.
        Placing of Tidball's Battery.

6.
Personal Narratives
of Participants

241   Adams, John G. B. _Reminiscenses of the Nineteenth Massachusetts Regiment_. Boston: Wright and Potter, 1899.

242   Allen, George H. _Forty Six Months with the Fourth R. I. Volunteers, in the War of 1861 to 1865_. Providence: J. A. & R. A. Reid:, 1887.
     Valuable work. Based upon Allen's wartime journal.

243   Alexander, Edward P. _Military Memoirs of a Confederate_. New York: C. Scribner's Sons, 1907.
     Oustanding critical narrative. Fine review of Confederate operations in Maryland.

244   Bartlett, John R. _Memoirs of Rhode Island Officers_. Providence: Rider, 1867.
     Contains some interesting personal accounts of Rhode Island officers at Antietam.

245   Bartlett, Napier. _A Soldier's Story of the War_. New Orleans: Clark & Hofeline, 1874.
     Bartlett served in the Washington Artillery. Fine description of the desperate action at the Piper Farm.

246   Bassett, Edward H. _From Bull Run to Bristoe Station_. St. Paul:Central Publishing Co., 1962.
     The author served in the 1st Minnesota.

247   Battle, Laura Elizabeth L. _Forget-Me-Nots of the Civil War: A Romance, Containing Reminiscences and Original Letters of Two Confederate Soldiers_. St. Louis: A. R. Fleming, 1909.
     Contains descriptive letter from Walter Lee of the 4th North Carolina concerning action at the Piper Farm.

248   Baylor, George. _Bull Run to Bull Run; or Four Years in the Army of Northern Virginia_. Richmond: B. F. Johnson, 1900.
     Fine memoir of service in the Confederate cavalry.

249   Beale, George W. _A Lieutenant of Cavalry in Lee's
Army_. Boston: The Gorham Press, 1918.
        A rather detached account of Stuart's Cavalry, the 9th
Virginia in particular, during the Maryland Campaign.

250   Benson, Susan W., ed. _Berry Benson's Civil War Book:
Memoirs of a Confederate Scout and Sharpshooter_. Athens:
Univ. of Georgia Press, 1962.
        Benson served in Gregg's South Carolina Brigade. Good
description of A. P. Hill's counterattack upon Burnside's
9th Corps.

251   Berkeley, Henry R. _Four Years in the Confederate
Artillery; The Diary of Private Henry Robinson Berkeley_.
Chapel Hill:Univ. of North Carolina Press, 1961.
        Berkeley's battery was broken up before the army
entered Maryland. However, the diary contains some useful
information about the Confederate artillery.

252   Bernard, George S. _War Talks of Confederate Veterans_.
Petersburg: Penn and Owen, 1892.
        Contains invaluable personal reminiscences of the
Battle of Crampton's Gap from veterans of Mahone's
Virginia Brigade. Limited Antietam information.

253   Beyer, W. F. and Keydel, O. F. _Deeds of Valor; How
America's Heroes Won the Medal of Honor_. 2 vols. Detroit:
Perrien-Keydel, 1906.
        Superb, though possibly somewhat embellished, accounts
of Union soldiers heroism that earned them the Medal of
Honor.

254   Blackford, William W. _War Years With Jeb Stuart_.
New York: Charles Scribner's Sons, 1946.
        Many anecdotes and personal incidents of Blackford's
service in Maryland while on Stuart's staff.

255   Bloss, John M. "Antietam and the Lost Dispatch," _War
Papers_, I, (Commandery of the State of Kansas, MOLLUS.)
Kansas City, MO: Franklin Hudson Publishing House, 1906.
        Bloss was one of the men who discovered S.O. 191 at
Frederick.

256   Borcke, Heros von. _Memoirs of the Confederate War for
Independence_. Edinburgh and London: W. Blackford & Sons,
1866.
        Von Borcke was on Stuart's staff. Valuable details on
Stuart in Maryland, particularly at Crampton's Gap.

257   Brown, Philip F. _Reminiscences of the War, 1861 –
1865_. Blue Ridge Springs, Va.: By the Author, 1912.
        Valuable personal account of Crampton's Gap from a
member of the 12th Virginia, Mahone's Brigade.

258   Brown, Varina D. _A Colonel at Gettysburg and
Spotsylvania_. Columbia, SC: The State Company, 1931.

A military biography of Colonel Joseph N. Brown, 14th
South Carolina. Contains a useful wartime letter of
Brown's describing Antietam.

259   Buell, Augustus. "The Cannoneer." Recollections of
Service in the Army of the Potomac. Washington, D.C.: The
National Tribune, 1890.
        Battery B, 4th U.S. Although superbly detailed, the
author was not with the battery at Antietam. Only value
is letters concerning Antietam from veterans to the
author.

260   Burkhardt, A. W. Forty Hours on the Battlefield of
Antietam: Or The Foeman Friend. n.p.,n.d.
        Concerns the 16th Connecticut at Antietam.

261   Byrne, Frank L., ed. Haskell of Gettysburg: His Life
and Civil War Papers. Madison: State Historical Society
of Wisconsin, 1970.
        Staff officer with Gibbon's Iron Brigade. Contains
Haskell's observant letters describing South Mountain and
Antietam.

262   Canfield, William A. A History of the Army Experience
of William A. Canfield. Manchester, NH: Charles F.
Livingston, 1869.
        Brief history of Canfield's wartime experiences with
the 9th New Hampshire. This regiment saw action at both
South Mountain and Antietam.

263   Carter, Robert G. Four Brothers in Blue; Or, Sunshine
and Shadows of the War of the Rebellion; A Story of the
Great Civil War from Bull Run to Appomattox. Austin:
University of Texas Press, 1978.
        Weaves narrative and letters together. Robert Carter
served at Antietam with the 22nd Massachusetts. Useful
material.

264   Carter, Sindey. Dear Bet: The Carter Letters, 1861-
1863: The Letters of Lieutenant Sindey Carter, Company A,
14th Regiment, South Carolina Volunteers, Gregg's
McGowen's Brigade, CSA, to Ellen Timmons Carter. Clemson,
SC: B. M. Lane, 1978.

265   Casler, John O. Four Years in the Stonewall Brigade.
Guthrie, OK: Oklahoma State Capitol Printing Co.,
1893.
        Outstanding personal account. Cursory treatment of
Maryland Campaign.

266   Chamberlaine, William W. Memoirs of the Civil War.
Washington, D. C.: Byron S. Adams, 1912.
        Served as a Lieutenant in the 6th Virginia. Excellent
desription of the Piper Farm action from a unit with
little other published material.

267   Chamberlayne, John H. Ham Chamberlayne--Virginia
Letters and Papers of an Artillery Officer in the War for
Southern Independence, 1861-1865. Richmond: Dietz
Printing Co. , 1932.
    Although not so useful for the Battle of Antietam,
quite good for an articulate, observant Confederate
soldier's observations of Maryland in September, 1862.

268   Coco, Gregory A. Through Blood and Fire: The Civil War
Letters of Major Charles J. Mills, 1862-1865. Privately
Printed, 1982.
    The letters of an intelligent and witty Lieutenant
from the 2nd Mass. Infantry. Was severely wounded at
Antietam.

269   Coffin, Charles C. The Boys of '61: Or, Four Years of
Fighting. A Record of Personal Observation with the Army
and Navy From the First Battle of Bull Run to the Fall of
Richmond. Boston: Estes & Lauriat, 1881.

270   Cole, Jacob. Under Five Commanders; Or, A Boy's
Experience With the Army of the Potomac. Patterson, NJ:
News Printing Co., 1905.
    An officer with the 57th New York. Vivid description
of the fighting at the Sunken Lane.

271   Commager, Henry S. The Blue and Gray; The Story of the
Civil War As Told by the Participant. 2 vols.
Indianapolis: Bobbs-Merrill, 1950.
    A useful compilation of previously published eye-
witness accounts.

272   Cox, Jacob D. Military Reminiscences of the Civil War.
New York: Charles Scribner's Sons, 1900.
    Outstanding, objective, personal narrative of the
Maryland Campaign by the temporary commander of the 9th
Corps. Also see his articles on South Mountain and
Antietam in Battles and Leaders.

273   Crary, Catherine S., ed. Dear Belle; Letters from a
Cadet & Officer to His Sweetheart. Middletown, CT:
Wesleyan University Press, 1965.
    Letters of Union artillerymen Tully McRea. Good
description of Confederate counterattack that followed
Sedgwick's repulse.

274   Davis, Nicholas A. Chaplain Davis and Hood's Texas
Brigade. San Antonio, TX: Principle Press of Trinity
University, 1962.
    Useful information, but use with some caution as Davis
offers some opinions based upon hearsay.

275   Dawson, Francis W. Reminiscences of Confederate
Service, 1861-1865. Charleston, SC: News and Courier Book
Presses, 1882.
    Dawson served at one time on Longstreet's staff.

Although he was not at Antietam, his observant commentary is worth consulting.

276   Douglas, Henry Kyd. I Rode With Stonewall. Chapel Hill, NC: University of North Carolina Press, 1940.
      Filled with fascinating details concerning the actions of Jackson's command by a member of his staff.

277   Duncan, William M. War Letters of Andrew Jackson Duncan of Portland, Ohio, 1861-1865. Detroit: Cadillac Press, 1932.
      Duncan served in the 23rd Ohio.

278   Durkin, Joseph T., ed. John Dooley: Confederate Soldier; Or The Forefront of Battle. Little Rock, Ark.: Tunnah and Pittard, 1899.
      A fresh, honest narrative that offers fine personal accounts of South Mountain and Antietam by a member of the 1st Virginia Infantry.

279   Dwight, Wilder. Life and Letters of Wilder Dwight. Boston: Little, Brown, 1891.
      Observant, detailed letters by a Harvard educated officer. The last written during the Battle of Antietam as Dwight lay mortally wounded.

280   Eby, Cecil D. A Virginia Yankee in the Civil War: The Diaries of David Hunter Strother. Chapel Hill: University of North Carolina Press, 1961.
      Colonel Strother served on McClellan's staff. His diary entries are an invaluable look into McClellan's headquarters during the Maryland Campaign.

281   Eggelston, George Cary. A Rebel's Recollections. New York: G. P. Putnam's, 1905.

282   Faller, Leo W. Dear Folks at Home; The Civil War Letter of Leo W. and John I. Faller, with an Account of Andersonville. Carlisle, PA: Cumberland County Historical Society, 1963.
      Contains a rather brief letter describing the action of Meade's Division at South Mountain.

283   Favill, Joseph M. The Diary of a Young Officer. Chicago: R. R. Donnelly and Sons, 1909.
      Fine narrative by an officer of the 57th New York who was in the thick of the action at the sunken lane.

284   Figg, Royall W. "Where Only Men Dare To Go!" Or, The Story of a Boy Company (C.S.A). Richmond: Whittet & Shepperson, 1885.
      Parker's Virginia Battery. Useful narrative of the battery's service at Antietam.

285   Fiske, Samuel W. Dunn Browne's Experience in the Army. Boston: Nichols and Noyes, 1866.

Dunn Browne was Fiske's pen name. Served in the 14th Connecticut and saw heavy action at the sunken lane. Fine memoir.

286   Fuller, Charles A. Personal Recollections of War of 1861. Sherburne, NY: News Job Printing House, 1906.
Excellent front line material of the sunken lane struggle by a member of the 61st New York.

287   Galwey, Thomas F. The Valiant Hours: Narrative of "Captain Brevet," an Irish-American in the Army of the Potomac. Harrisburg, PA: Stackpole, 1961.
A sergeant in the 8th Ohio graphically describes the sunken lane fighting.

288   Gibbon, John. Personal Recollections of the Civil War. New York, London: G. P. Putnam, 1928.
Reliable, straightforward account of South Mountain and Antietam by the commander of the Iron Brigade.

289   Glover, Robert W., ed. Tyler to Sharpsburg by Robert H. and William H. Gaston, Their War Letters, 1861-1865. Waco, TX: W. M. Morrison, 1960.
Authors of letters served in Hood's Texas Brigade.

290   Goss, Warren Lee. Recollections of a Private: A Story of the Army of the Potomac. New York: Thomas Y. Crowell, 1890.
Entertaining memoir by a member of the 5th New Hampshire.

291   Gould, John Mead. Joseph K. Mansfield, Brigadier General of the U. S. Army. A Narrative of Events Connected with His Mortal Wounding at Antietam, Sharpsburg, Maryland, September 17, 1862. Portland, ME: S. Berry, 1895.
An excellent pamphlet that looks at who shot Mansfield. Many personal observations of 12th Corps action in East Woods.

292   Govan, Gilbert E., and Livingood, James W. The Haskell Memoirs; The Personal Narrative of a Confederate Officer. New York: G. P. Putnam's Sons, 1960.
Memoirs of John Cheeves Haskell. Was not at Antietam but offers many useful sketches of various Confederate officers who were.

293   Gray, John C. War Letters, 1862-1865, of John Chipman Gray...and John Codman Ropes...With Portraits. New York: Houghton Mifflin, 1927.
Contains fine descriptive letter from Gray describing a visit to Antietam several weeks after the battle.

294   Hall, H. Seymour. "Personal Experiences Under General
        McClellan, after Bull Run, Including the Peninsular and
        Antietam Campaigns July 27, 1861 to Nov. 10, 1862," War
        Papers, II, (Commandery of the State of Kansas, MOLLUS.)
        n.p., n.d.

295   Hassler, William W. The General to his Lady; The Civil
        War Letter of William Dorsey Pender to Fanny Pender.
        Chapel Hill: University of North Carolina Press, 1965.
            Although Pender does not offer much on Antietam, his
        letters provide some isolated bits of information on the
        Confederate army in Maryland.

296   Haynes, Draughton S. The Field Diary of a Confederate
        Soldier...While Serving With the Army of Northern
        Virginia. Darien, GA: Ashantilly Press, 1963.
            Haynes served in the 49th Georgia of A. P. Hill's
        Division. Brief entries but contains some material of
        interest.

297   Hays, John. The 130 Regiment Pennsylvania Volunteers
        in the Maryland Campaign. Carlisle, PA: Herald Printing
        Co., 1894.
            An address delivered to a G.A.R. post. Personal
        experiences.

298   Hill, A. F. Our Boys. The Personal Experience of a
        Soldier in the Army of the Potomac. Philadelphia: John F.
        Potter, 1866.
            By a member of the Pennsylvania Reserves. Much
        dialogue and generally unreliable.

299   Hinkley, Julian W. A Narrative of Service with the
        Third Wisconsin Infantry. Madison, WI: Wisconsin History
        Commission, 1912.
            Well written and highly detailed narrative.

300   Hitchcock, Frederick L. War From the Inside or
        Personal Experiences, Impressions and Reminiscences of
        One of the "Boys" in the War of the Rebellion.
        Philadelphia: J. B. Lippincott, 1904.
            Narrative of the adjutant of the 130th Pennsylvania.
        Observant and highly detailed.

301   Hopkins, Luther W. From Bull Run to Appomattox: A
        Boy's View. Baltimore: Fleet-McGinley Co., 1908.
            6th Virginia Cavalry.

302   Howe, Mark DeWolfe, ed. Touched With Fire: Civil War
        Letters and Diary of Oliver Wendell Holmes, Jr. 1861-
        1864. Cambridge, MA: Harvard University Press, 1947.
            Holmes was a Lieutenant in the 20th Massachusetts. An
        Antietam letter describes his severe wounding in the West
        Woods.

303   Howard, Oliver O. *Autiobiography of Oliver Otis Howard*. New York: The Baker and Taylor Co., 1907.
A fairly straightforward and even-tempered account of Antietam, where Howard commanded the Philadelphia Brigade in Sedgwick's Division.

304   Hunter, Alexander. *Johnny Reb and Billy Yank*. New York: Neale Publishing, 1905.
A private in the 17th Virginia. Although much of the dialogue is invented, there is plenty of valuable information within.

305   Hunton, Eppa. *Autobiography of Eppa Hunton*. Richmond: The William Byrd Press Inc., 1933.
Memoirs of the Colonel of the 8th Virginia. Served at South Mountain and Antietam.

306   Hyde, Thomas W. *Following the Greek Cross; Or, Memories of the Sixth Army Corps*. New York: Houghton Mifflin, 1894.
Fine memoir from an officer of the 7th Maine. Moving account of the regiment's ill-fated charge at Antietam.

307   Jackson, Edgar A. *Three Rebels Write Home*. Franklin, VA: News Publishing Co., 1955.

308   Johnson, Charles F. *The Long Roll: Being a Journal of the Civil War as Set Down During the Years 1861-1863, by...Sometime of Hawkins Zouaves*. Aurora, N.Y.: Roycroftens, 1911.
Excellent personal descriptions of both South Mountain and Antietam by a member of the 9th New York.

309   Johnston, David E. *The Story of a Confederate Boy in The Civil War*. Ann Arbor: University Microfilms, 1972.
Served in 7th Virginia. Useful account of South Mountain. Saw little action at Antietam.

310   Jones Evan R. *Four Years in the Army of the Potomac: A Soldier's Recollections*. London: Tyne Publishing, 1881.
Served in the 5th Wisconsin. Not much value on Maryland Campaign.

311   Kent, Arthur A., ed. *Three Years With Company K*. Rutherford, NJ: Dickinson University Press, 1976.
One of the frankest, freshest memoirs of a front line foot soldier in the war that has been published. 13th Massachusetts.

312   Lane, David. *A Soldier's Diary, 1862-1865: The Story of a Volunteer*. n.p. 1905.
A Private in the 17th Michigan. Describes experiences at South Mountain. Adequate of Antietam.

313   Lasswell, Mary, comp. and ed. Rags and Hope; The
Recollections of Val C. Giles, Four Years With Hood's
Brigade, Fourth Texas Infantry. New York: Coward-McCann,
1961.

314   Ledford, P. L. Reminiscences of the Civil War, 1861-
1865. Thomasville, NC: New Printing House, 1909.
         14th NC.

315   Leon, L. Diary of a Tar Heel Confederate Soldier.
Charlotte, NC: Stone, 1913.
         1st NC.

316   Letterman, Jonathan. Medical Recollections of the Army
of the Potomac. D. New York: Appleton and Co., 1866.
         Letterman was the medical director of the Army of the
Potomac at Antietam. Valuable for medical aspects of
campaign and battle.

317   Longstreet, James. From Manassas to Appomattox.
Philadelphia: J. B. Lippincott Co., 1896.
         Although colored somewhat by hindsight and personal
prejudice, Longstreet's account of the Maryland Campaign
is quite good. Also see his article for Battles and
Leaders.

318   Loving, Jerome M., ed. Civil War Letters of George
Washington Whitman. Durham: Duke University Press, 1975.
         Intelligent, observant letters describing both South
Mountain and Antietam by a member of the 51st New York.

319   Luff, William M. "March of the Cavalry From Harper's
Ferry Sept. 14, 1862," War Papers, II (Commandery of the
State of Illinois, MOLLUS.) Chicago: A. C. McClure, 1894.
         Concerns the escape of the federal cavalry from
Harper's Ferry.

320   Lyle, William W. Lights and Shadows of Army Life: Or,
Pen Pictures from the Battlefield, the Camp, and the
Hospital. Cincinnati: R. W. Carroll, 1865.
         Served with 11th Ohio. Not very useful.

321   McCain, General Warren. A Soldier's Diary; Or, the
History of Company "L," Third Indiana Cavalry.
Indianapolis: William A. Patton, 1885.

322   McClendon, William A. Recollections of War Times.
Montgomery, AL: Paragon Press, 1909.
         15th Alabama. Rather superficial treatment of campaign
and battle.

323   McClenthen, Charles S. A Sketch of the Campaign in
Virginia and Maryland from Cedar Mountain to Antietam.
Syracuse: Masters and Lee, 1862.
         26th New York. Good descriptive account.

324   Maurice, Frederic, ed. An Aide-de-Camp of Lee, Being
the Papers of Colonel Charles Marshall Sometime Aide-de-
Camp, Military Secretary, and Assistant Adjutant General
on the Staff of Robert E. Lee, 1862-1865. Boston: Little,
Brown, 1927.

325   Meade, George G. Life and Letters of George Gordon
Meade. New York: C. Scribner's & Sons, 1913.
       Several brief, but valuable letters on the Maryland
Campaign by the commander of the Pennsylvania Reserves.

326   Mixon, Frank M. Reminiscences of a Private. Columbia,
SC: The State Co., 1910.
       1st South Carolina. A rare account from a unit with
little published. Unfortunately, Mixon's memory is not
trustworthy.

327   Moore, Edward A. The Story of a Cannoneer under
Stonewall Jackson. New York: Neale Publishing Co., 1907.
       Richly detailed personal observations by a member of
the Rockbridge Artillery.

328   Morse, Charles F. Letters Written During the Civil
War, 1861-1865. Boston: Privately Printed, 1898.
       Observant and informant letters from an intelligent
officer who served in the 2nd Massachusetts Infantry.

329   Neese, George M. Three Years in the Confederate Horse
Artillery. New York: Neale Publishing, 1911.
       Chew's Battery, Stuart's Horse Artillery. Contains
some interesting information on Crampton's Gap.

330   Nevins, Allan. A Diary of Battle; The Personal
Journals of Colonel Charles S. Wainwright. New York:
Harcourt, Brace & World, 1962.
       Wainwright just missed Antietam, but he re-joined army
the day after. His superb diary contains much
perceptive and illuminating information on the battle.

331   Nichols, G. W. A Soldier's Story of His Regiment.
Kennesaw, GA: Continental Book Co., 1961.
       Nichols served in the 61st Georgia of Lawton's Brigade
and fought near Miller's Cornfield. His account of battle
is quite brief.

332   Nisbet, James C. Four Years on the Firing Line.
Hackson, TN: McCowat-Mercer Press, 1963.
       Antietam from the viewpoint of a line officer in the
21st Georgia. Not that descriptive but contains some
valuable information.

333   Norton, Oliver W. Army Letters 1861 - 1865. Chicago:
O. L. Deming , 1903.
       Norton served with the 83rd Penna. in the 5th Corps.
Not much on Antietam but some on Sheperdstown.

334   Noyes, George F. The Bivouac and the Battlefield; Or,
Campaign Sketches in Virginia and Maryland. New York:
Harper and Brothers, 1863.
        Commissary officer in the Union 1st Corps. Classic
account of the 1st Corps at South Mountain. Missed heavy
action at Antietam.

335   Patrick, Marsena R. Inside Lincoln's Army. New York:
T. Yoseloff, 1964.
        The irascible, opinionated Patrick commanded a brigade
in Hooker's 1st Corps. His diary is invaluable.

336   Pattison, Everett. Some Personal Reminiscences of Army
Life. St. Louis: Smith & Owens, 1887.
        Served with 2nd Mass. Infantry.

337   Paver, John M. What I Saw From 1861 to 1864: Personal
Recollections of .... Indianapolis: Scott-Miller, 1906.
        A shallow memoir by an officer in the 5th Ohio.

338   Poague, William T. Gunner With Stonewall;
Reminiscences of William Thomas Poague, A Memoir, Written
for His Children in 1903. Jackson, TN: McCowat-Mercer
Press, 1957.
        Clearly written memoir by a forward battery commander
in Jackson's Corps at Antietam.

339   Polley, Joseph Benjamin. A Soldier's Letters to
Charming Nellie. New York and Washington: Neale
Publishing C., 1908.
        Polley served in Hood's Texas Brigade. However, Polley
may have written these letters after the war making their
value dubious.

340   Quaife, Milo, ed. From the Cannon's Mouth; The Civil
War Letters of Alpheus S. Williams. Detroit: Wayne State
University Press and Detroit Historical Society, 1959.
        Outstanding letters from the man who assumed command
of the 12th Corps after Mansfield's mortal wounding. A
mine of information concerning the 12th Corps.

341   Quint, Alonzo H. The Potomac and the Rapidan: Army
Notes from the Failure at Winchester to the Reinforcement
of Rosecrans, 1861-1863. Boston: Crosby and Nichols,
1864.
        Quint was a chaplain in the 2d Mass. Infantry. What
battle information he relates was gained second hand.

342   Reno, Conrad. "General Jesse L. Reno at Frederick,
Barbara Fritchie and Her Flag," War Papers, I,
(Commandery of the State of Massachusetts, MOLLUS.)
Boston, 1900.
        Reno's son writes about his father's experiences when
the 9th Corps entered Frederick.

343   Roulhac, J. G. de, ed. The Papers of Randolph Abbott
Shotwell. 2 vols. Raleigh, NC: North Carolina Historical
Commission, 1929-1931.
         Shotwell served with the 8th Virginia. Papers include
his descriptive diary.

344   Runge, William H., ed. Four Years in the Confederate
Artillery; The Diary of Private Henry Robinson Berkely.
Chapel Hill, NC: University of North Carolina Press for
the Virginia Historical Society, 1961.
         Although Berkely's battery was disbanded on the eve of
the Maryland Campaign, his diary is richly descriptive on
leadership and organization of CSA artillery.

345   Small, Harold Abner, ed. The Road to Richmond: The
Civil War Memoirs of Major Abner R. Small of the
Sixteenth Maine Volunteers, Together with the Diary Which
he kept When he was a Prisoner of War. Berkeley:
University of California Press, 1939.
         Fine description of the painful learning process a raw
regiment goes through in Maryland.

346   Spangler, Edward W. My Little War Experience. York,
PA: York Daily Publishing Co., 1904.
         Descriptive account of the 130th Penna. baptism of fire
at the Sunken Lane.

347   Stearns, Austin. Three Years With Company K.
Rutherford, NJ: Farliegh Dickinson University Press,
1976.
         A wonderfully frank account of army life. Describes
bloody fighting in the Miller Cornfield. 13th
Massachusetts.

348   Stewart, Alexander M. Camp, March and Battlefield; Or,
Three Years and a Half in the Army of the Potomac.
Philadelphia: J. B. Rogers, 1865.
         Author was a chaplain with the 13th PA Reserve, which
saw action at South Mountain and on the 16th and 17th of
September.

349   Stone, James Madison. Personal Recollections of the
Civil War. Boston: By The Author, 1918.
         A well written account of the author's experiences
with the 21st Mass. Infantry during the Maryland
Campaign.

350   Strong, George Templeton. Diary of the Civil War,
1860-1865. New York: Macmillan, 1962.
         Head of the Sanitary Commission. Some interesting
entries concerning McClellan.

351   Talcott, Philo F. Reminiscences of ... n.p., n.d.
         A rare volume concerning Talcott's service with 21st
Mass.

352   Taylor, Walter H. Four Years With General Lee. New
York: D. Appleton, 1962.
       Taylor did not accompany Lee through Maryland,
nevertheless, his account of Antietam is worth consulting.

353   _____. General Lee, His Campaigns in Virginia, 1861-
1865, With Personal Reminiscence. Brooklyn: Braunwroth
and Co., 1906.
       A more valuable work since it contains personal
observations.

354   Toombs, Samuel. Reminiscences of the War. Orange, NJ:
Journal Office, 1878.
       A well done narrative of Toombs service with the 13th
New Jersey, which saw its first action at Antietam with
the 12th Corps.

355   Vanderslice, Catherine H., ed. The Civil War Letters
of George Washington Beidleman. New York: Vantage, 1978.
       Beidleman served with the 71st Pennsylvania. Contains
a useful letter describing Sedgwick's defeat in the West
Woods.

356   Wagstaff, H. M., ed. The James A. Graham Papers, 1861-
1884. Chapel Hill: University of North Carolina Press,
1928.
       Graham was in the 27th North Carolina. Excellent
descriptive letter of the 27th's role in the battle.

357   Walton, William, ed. A Civil War Courtship: The
Letters of Edwin Weller from Antietam to Atlanta.
Garden City: Doubleday, 1980.
       Weller was in the 107th New York. His Antietam letter
is mediocre in quality.

358   Welch, Spencer Glasglow. A Confederate Surgeon's
Letters to His Wife. Marietta, GA: Continental, 1954.
       Welch was a surgeon with the 13th South Carolina.
Little detail on his work at Antietam.

359   Weld, Stephen Minot. War Diary and Letters of Stephen
Minot Weld, 1861-1865. Cambridge, MA: Riverside Press, 1912.
       Weld was a staf officer for 5th Corps Commander, Fitz
John Porter.

360   Williams, Charles R. Diary and Letters of Rutherford
B. Hayes. Columbus, OH: Ohio State Archaeological and
Historical Society, 1922-1926.
       Hayes commanded the 23rd Ohio at South Mountain, where
he was wounded. His diary and letters describing action
are among the best personal accounts of South Mountain.

361   Wistar, Isaac Jones. Autobiography of Isaac Jones
Wistar, 1827-1905; Half a Century in War and Peace.
Philadelphia: Wistar Institute of Anatomy and Biology,
1937.

Wistar's Civil War section is brief, but his description of service as Colonel of the 71st Pennsylvania with Sedgwick in the West Woods is excellent.

362   Wood, James H. _The War: "Stonewall" Jackson. His Campaigns and Battles. The Regiment as I Saw Them_. Eddy Press: Cumberland, MD, 1911.
        37th Virginia. Not very valuable for Maryland Campaign.

363   Wood, William Nathaniel. _Reminiscences of Big I_. Jackson, TN: McCowat-Mercer Press, 1956.
        Wood was a Lieutenant in the 19th Virginia. Useful personal observations of South Mountain and Antietam.

364   Worsham, John H. _One of Jackson's Foot Cavalry: His Experience and What He Saw During the War, 1861-1865_. New York: Neale Publishing, 1912.
        A classic Confederate foot soldier's account.

7.
Union Unit Histories

ARMY LEVEL

365   McClellan, George B. The Army of the Potomac: Report
of Its Operations While Under His Command, With Maps and
Plans. New York: G. P. Putnam, 1864.
        McClellan's "official" story of his command of the
army. Nothing that was not published in the Offical
Records.

366   Naisawald, L. Van Loan. Grape and Canister: The Story
of the Field Artillery of the Army of the Potomac. Oxford
& New York: University Press, 1960.
        Well written but uses few unpublished manuscripts.
Good analysis of shortcomings of Union artillery at
Antietam.

367   Stine, James H. History of the Army of the Potomac.
Washington, D.C.: Gibson, 1893.
        Nothing new.

368   Swinton, William. Campaigns of the Army of the
Potomac: A Critical History of Operations in Virginia,
Maryland and Pennsylvania from the Commencement to the
Close of the War, 1861-1865. New York: Charles Scribers,
1881.
        A good, useful history. Relatively even-handed.

CORPS LEVEL

369   Powell, William H. The Fifth Army Corps: A Record of
Operations During the Civil War in the United States of
America, 1861 - 1865. New York: G. P. Putnam's Sons,
1896.
        One of the better corps histories.

370   Walker, Francis A. History of the Second Army Corps in
the Army of the Potomac. New York: Charles Scribners,
1886.
         Good overview of 2nd Corps operations at Antietam by a
former staff officer of the corps.

BRIGADE LEVEL

371   Auberry, C. Echoes From the Marches of the Iron
Brigade. Ann Arbor: University Microfilms, 1973.
         A compilation of various anecdotes relating to the
Iron Brigade during the war.

372   Banes, Charles H. History of The Philadelphia Brigade.
Philadelphia: J. B. Lippincott, 1876.
         Straightforward operations. Personal observations are
rare.

373   Conyngham, David P. The Irish Brigade and Its
Campaigns: With Some Account of the Corcoran Legion and
Sketches of its Principal Officers. Boston: P. Donhoe,
1869.
         Mediocre account of the Irish Brigade in combat at the
Sunken Lane.

374   Hough, Franklin B. History of Duryee's Brigade During
the Campaign in Virginia Under Gen. Pope and in Maryland
Under Gen. McClellan in the Summer and Autumn of 1862.
ALbany, N.Y.: J. Munsell, 1864.
         Rather superficial account of Duryee's operations at
South Mountain and Antietam.

375   Nolan, Allan. The Iron Brigade. Madison; State
Historical Society of Wisconsin, 1975.
         Fine modern history of a famous fighting unit.

REGIMENTAL LEVEL

CONNECTICUT

376   Connecticut. Record of Service of Connecticut Men in
the Army and Navy of the United States During the War of
the Rebellion. Hartford, CT.: Case, Lockwood and
Brainard, 1889.
         Contains the rosters of all Connecticut units in the
war. Invaluable for tracking down information on
individuals, composition of companies, final killed in
action, etc.

377   Marvin, Edwin E. The Fifth Regiment Connecticut
Volunteers. Hartford, CT: Wiley, Waterman and Eaton,
1889.
         The 5th was left behind at Frederick. Contains some
early campaign information.

378   Goddard, Henry P. Fourteenth Regiment Connecticut
Volunteers: Regimental; Reminiscences. Middletown: C. W.
Church, 1877.

379   Page, Charles D. History of the Fourteenth Regiment
Connecticut Volunteer Infantry. Meriden: Horton
Publishing Co., 1906.
        Despite its rather late printing date, this is a fine
regimental history and contains rich details on their
action at the Sunken Lane.

380   Stevens, H. S. Souvenir of Excursions to Battlefields
by the Society of the Fourteenth Connecticut Regiment and
Reunion at Antietam, September, 1891. Washington, D. C.:
Gibson Brothers, 1873.
        Reminiscences of veterans and brief history of unit.

381   Blakeslee, B. F. History of the Sixteenth Connecticut
Volunteers. Hartford: Case, Lockwood and Brainard, 1875.
        Based upon the author's diary, consequently more a
personal narrative than a unit history.

382   Burkhardt, A. W. Forty Hours on the Battlefield of
Antietam: Or, the Foeman Friend. n.p., n.d.
        The experiences of a soldier in the 16th Conn. who was
wounded in the 40 acre cornfield.

DELAWARE

383   Murphy, Thomas G. Four Years in the War: The History
of the First Regiment of Deleware Veteran Volunteers.
Philadelphia: James S. Claxton, 1866.

384   Seville, William P. History of the First Regiment
Delaware Volunteers. Wilmington: Historical Society of
Delaware, 1884.

385   Smith, Robert G. A Brief Account of the Services
Rendered by the Second Delaware Volunteers in the War of
the Rebellion. Wilmington: Historical Society of
Delaware, 1909.
        Very disappointing.

ILLINOIS

386   Hard, Abner. History of the Eight Cavalry Regiment,
Illinois Volunteers, During the Great Rebellion. Aurora:
By the Author, 1868.
        Particularly good on McClellan's pursuit of Lee from
South Mountain and the cavalry combat in Boonsborough.

INDIANA

387   Merril, Catherine. <u>The Soldier of Indiana in the War</u>
<u>for the Union</u>. 2 Vols. Indianapolis, Ind.: Merrill and
Co., 1866-69.
Volume 1 contains the engaged strengths of Indiana
units at Antietam.

388   Brown, Edmund R. <u>The Twenty-Seventh Indiana Volunteer</u>
<u>Infantry in the War of the Rebellion, 1861-1865, First</u>
<u>Division, XII and XX Corps</u>. n.p., 1899.
An outstanding regimental. Excellent description of
the 27th's grim combat near Miller's cornfield.

389   Pickerill, William N. <u>History of the 3rd Indiana</u>
<u>Cavalry</u>. Indianapolis: Aetna Printing Co., 1906.
Poor regimental history. Hardly worth consulting on
Maryland Campaign.

MAINE

390   Gould, John Mead. <u>History of the First - Tenth -</u>
<u>Twenty Ninth Maine Regiment</u>. Portland: Stephen Berry,
1871.
Gould was the adjutant of the 10th Maine at Antietam.
He consulted many fellow veterans in writing this
history.

391   Bicknell, George W. <u>History of the Fifth Maine</u>
<u>Volunteers</u>. Portland: Hall L. Davis, 1871.

392   Clark, Charles A. <u>Campaigning With the Sixth Maine</u>.
Des Moines: Kenyon Press, 1897.
The 6th saw limited action with the 6th Corps in the
Maryland Campaign.

393   Small, Abner R. <u>The Sixteenth Maine in the War of the</u>
<u>Rebellion</u>. Portland: Thurston Print, 1900.
Although the 16th was not engaged in Maryland, Small
provides a picture of the painful process a green
regiment had to endure in becoming soldiers.

394   Merrill, Samuel H. <u>The Campaigns of the First Maine</u>
<u>and First District of Columbia Cavalry</u>. Portland: Baily
and Hayes, 1866.

395   Tobie, Edward P. <u>History of the First Maine Cavalry,</u>
<u>1861-1865</u>. Boston: Emery and Hughes, 1887.
A huge, immensely detailed regimental history.

MARYLAND

396   Maryland. Commission on the Publication of the
Histories of the Maryland Volunteers During the Civil
War. History and Roster of Maryland Volunteers, War of
1861-5. 2 Vols. Baltimore: Press of Guggenheimer, Well &
Co., 1889-1890.

397   Newcomer, C. Armour. Cole's Cavalry; Or Three Years in
the Saddle in The Shenandoah Valley. Baltimore: Cashing
and Co., 1895.
        Despite some errors and a mediocre text, some valuable
information on the federal cavalry escape from Harper's
Ferry can be gleaned.

MASSACHUSETTS

398   Massachusetts. Adjutant General's Office.
Massachusetts Soldiers, Sailors and Marines in the Great
Civil War. 8 vols. Norwood: Norwood Press, 1931.

399   Gordon, George H. History of the 2nd Massachusetts
Regiment in the War of the Great Rebellion, 1861-1862.
Boston: Alfred Mudge and Son, 1885.
        Superior to Quint's history of the regiment. Gordon
commanded a brigade at Antietam, which 2d Mass. was
attached to.

400   Quint, Alonzo. The Record of the 2nd Massachusetts
Regiment Infantry, 1861-1865. Boston: James P. Walker,
1867.
        Quint was the regiments chaplain. A fair history of
the regiment with some description of the regiment at
Antietam.

401   Cook, Benjamin F. History of the Twelfth Massachusetts
Volunteers (Webster Regiment). Boston: Twelfth (Webster)
Regiment Association, 1882.
        The 12th suffered the highest regimental loss at
Antietam. Relies on diaries of various members of the
regiment. Thin on Antietam.

402   Davis, Charles E. Jr. Three Years in the Army. The
Story of the Thirteenth Massachusetts Volunteers From
July 16, 1861 to August 1, 1864. Boston: Estes and
Lauriat, 1894.
        A fine history and good description of the 13th's
action in Miller's Cornfield.

403   Earle, David M. History of the Excursion of the
Fifteenth Massachusetts Regiment and its Friends to the
Battlefields of Gettysburg, Pa., Antietam, Ball's Bluff,
Virginia, and Washington, D.C., May 31 - June 12, 1866.
Worcester: Charles Hamilton, 1886.

404   Ford, Andrew E. <u>The</u> <u>Story</u> <u>of</u> <u>the</u> <u>Fifteenth</u> <u>Regiment</u>
<u>Massachusetts</u> <u>Volunteer</u> <u>Infantry</u> <u>in</u> <u>the</u> <u>Civil</u> <u>War,</u> <u>1861-</u>
<u>1864</u>. Clinton: W. J. Coulter, 1898.
       Although not a particularly good regimental, it is
helpful for the 15th's service at Antietam.

405   Adams, John Gregory Bishop. <u>Reminiscences</u> <u>of</u> <u>the</u>
<u>Nineteenth</u> <u>Massachusetts</u> <u>Regiment</u>. Boston: Wright &
Potter, 1899.
       Adams' personal narrative of service with the 19th.

406   Waite, Ernest L, comp. <u>History</u> <u>of</u> <u>the</u> <u>Nineteenth</u>
<u>Regiment</u> <u>Massachusetts</u> <u>Volunteer</u> <u>Infantry,</u> <u>1861-1865</u>.
Salem: Salem Press Co., 1906.
       Fine description of the debacle that befell Sedgwick
in the West Wood.

407   Bruce, George A. <u>The</u> <u>Twentieth</u> <u>Regiment</u> <u>of</u>
<u>Massachusetts</u> <u>Volunteer</u> <u>Infantry</u>. New York: Houghton
Mifflin, 1906.
       Yet another viewpoint of Sedgwick's West Woods
disaster. Interesting look at Sumner's generalship and
state of mind.

408   Walcott, Charles F. <u>History</u> <u>of</u> <u>the</u> <u>Twenty-First</u>
<u>Regiment</u> <u>Massachusetts</u> <u>Volunteers</u> <u>in</u> <u>the</u> <u>War</u> <u>For</u> <u>the</u>
<u>Preservation</u> <u>of</u> <u>the</u> <u>Union,</u> <u>1861-1865</u>. Boston: Houghton
Mifflin, 1882.
       A straightforward narrative by a member of the
regiment.

409   Parker, John L., and Carter, Robert G. <u>History</u> <u>of</u> <u>the</u>
<u>Twenty-First</u> <u>Massachusetts</u> <u>Infantry,</u> <u>the</u> <u>Second</u> <u>Company</u>
<u>Sharpshooters,</u> <u>and</u> <u>the</u> <u>Third</u> <u>Light</u> <u>Battery</u> <u>in</u> <u>the</u> <u>Third</u>
<u>Light</u> <u>Battery</u> <u>in</u> <u>the</u> <u>War</u> <u>of</u> <u>the</u> <u>Rebellion</u>. Boston: Rand
Avery Co., 1887.

410   Osborne, William H. <u>The</u> <u>History</u> <u>of</u> <u>the</u> <u>Twenty-Ninth</u>
<u>Regiment</u> <u>of</u> <u>Massachusetts</u> <u>Volunteer</u> <u>Infantry,</u> <u>in</u> <u>the</u> <u>Late</u>
<u>War</u> <u>of</u> <u>the</u> <u>Rebellion</u>. Boston: Albert J. Wright, 1877.
       The 29th was attached to the Irish Brigade and saw
action at the Sunken Lane. Detailed with some personal
observations.

411   Parker, Francis J. <u>The</u> <u>Story</u> <u>of</u> <u>the</u> <u>Thirty-Second</u>
<u>Regiment</u> <u>Massachusetts</u> <u>Infantry</u>. Boston: C. W. Calkins,
1880.
       Excellent description of what the 5th Corps observed
of the battle.

412   No Author. <u>History</u> <u>of</u> <u>the</u> <u>Thirty-Fifth</u> <u>Regiment</u>
<u>Massachusetts</u> <u>Volunteers,</u> <u>1862-1865</u>. Boston: Mills,
Knight, and Co., 1884.
       A descriptive account of the 35th's part in the
Battles of South Mountain and Antietam.

413   Crowinshield, Benjamin W., and Leason, D. H. L.
<u>History</u> <u>of</u> <u>the</u> <u>First</u> <u>Regiment</u> <u>of</u> <u>Massachusetts</u> <u>Cavalry</u>
<u>Volunteers</u>. Boston and New York: Houghton Mifflin, 1891.
       Highly detailed on regiment's participation in the
campaign.

414   Bennett, Andrew J. The Story of the First
Massachusetts Light Battery, Attached to the Sixth Army
Corps. Boston: Deland and Barts, 1886.

415   Parker, John Lord. Henry Wilson's Regiment. Boston:
Press of Rand and Avery, 1887.
        The 3rd Massachusetts Light Battery.

MICHIGAN

416   Brown, Ida C. Michigan in the Civil War. 2 vols. Ann
Arbor: University of Michigan, 1966.
        Some material on the 7th and 17th Michigan.

417   Michigan. Record of Service of Michigan Volunteers in
the Civil War. 46 vols. Kalamazoo: Ihling Brothers and
Everhard, 1903.

418   Tivy, Joseph A. Souvenir of the Seventh Containing a
Brief History of It. Detroit: By the Author, 1893.
        7th Infantry. Superficial treatment of Antietam.

MINNESOTA

419   Minnesota. Board of Commissioners on Publication of
History of Minnesota in Civil and Indian Wars. Minnesota
in the Civil and Indian Wars, 1861-1865. 2 vols. St.
Paul: Pioneer Press Company, 1890-1893.
        Contains a short history of the 1st Minnesota with
some valuable information on the 1st at Antietam.

420   No Author. History of the First Regiment Minnesota
Volunteer Infantry, 1861-1864. Stillwater: Easton &
Masterman, 1916.

NEW HAMPSHIRE

421   Waite, Otis F. R. New Hampshire in the Great
Rebellion. Claremont, NH: Tracy, Chase and Co., 1870.

422   Jackman, Lyman, and Hadley, Ancos. History of the
Sixth New Hampshire Regiment in the War for the Union.
Concord: Ira C. Evans, 1896.
        Based upon Jackman's diary with personal recollections
from members of the regiment.

423   Lord, Edward O. History of the Ninth Regiment New
Hampshire Volunteers in the War of the Rebellion.
Concord: Republican Press Association, 1895.
        Excellent regimental. Contains recollections of many
regimental members on South Mountain and Antietam.

424   New Hampshire. Names and Records of All the Members
Who Served in the First N. H. Battery of Light Artillery.
Manchester: Budget Job Print, 1891.
        Nothing but the roster of Edgell's Battery.

NEW JERSEY

425   New Jersey. Records of Officers and Men of New Jersey
in the Civil War 1861-1865. 2 vols. Trenton: John L.
Murphy, 1876.

426   No Author. Historical Sketch of Co. "D". New York: D.
H. Gildersleeve, 1875.
       An unusually honest memoir of a company from the 13th
New Jersey.

427   Toombs, Samuel. Reminiscences of the War, Comprising
a Detailed Account of the Experiences of the Thirteenth
Regiment New Jersey Volunteers in Camp, on the March, and
in Battle. Orange: Journal Office, 1878.

428   Terrill, John Newton. Campaign of the Fourteenth
Regiment New Jersey Volunteers. New Brunswick: Daily
House News Press, 1884.
       The 14th was stationed at the Baltimore and Ohio
railroad bridge over the Moncacy River during the opening
phases of the Confederate invasion.

NEW YORK

429   New York. A Record of the Commissioned Officers, Non-
Commissioned Officers and Privates, of the Regiments
Which Were Organized in the State of New York. 8 vols.
Albany: Comstock and Cassidy, 1864.

430   Phisterer, Frederick. New York in the War of The
Rebellion 1861-1865. Albany: Weed, Parsons and Co., 1890.
       A very useful set. Contains a short descriptive
roster of every New York officer, the casualties, by
battle, of every regiment, and a brief narrative of
service.

431   New York State. Monuments Commission for the
Battlefield of Gettysburg, Chattanooga and Antietam. New
York at Antietam. Albany: J. B. Lyon, 1923.
       Partially concerned with dedication of New York State
Memorial. Also contains an excellent narrative covering
the entire Maryland campaign.

432   Davenport, Alfred. Camp and Field Life of the Fifth
New York Volunteer Infantry. New York: Dick and
Fitzgerald, 1879.
       The 5th was not engaged at Antietam, being held in
reserve.

433   Graham, Matthew. The Ninth Regiment New York
Volunteers. New York: E. P. Coby and Co., 1900.
       Based principally on printed sources, although there
is some good material on the 9th at Antietam.

434   Whitney, J. H. E. The Hawkins Zouaves: (Ninth N.Y.)
Their Battles and Marches. New York: By the Author, 1866.

Weak on service at South Mountain and Antietam.

435   Cowtan, Charles W. Services of the Tenth New York
Volunteers in the War of the Rebellion. New York: Charles
H. Ludwig, 1882.
    Standard regimental. Little personal insight or
observations.

436   Tevis, C. V. The History of the Fighting Fourteenth.
n.p., 1911.
    History of the 14th Brooklyn (84th New York). A poor
unit history although some basic information on the 14th
at Antietam can be drawn out.

437   Curtis, Newton Martin. From Bull Run to
Chancellorsville: The Story of the Sixteenth New York
Infantry Together With Personal Reminiscences. New York:
G. P. Putnam, 1906.
    The Maryland Campaign section principally deals with
the author's experiences with the ambulance corps at
Battle of Crampton's Gap.

438   Thompson, William M. Historical Sketch of the
Sixteenth Regiment N.Y.S. Volunteer Infantry, April 1861
- May 1863. First Reunion, August 31, September 1, 1886.
Potsdam: n.p., 1886.

439   Mills, J. Harrison. Chronicles of the Twenty-First
Regiment New York State Volunteers. Buffalo: 21st
Regimental Association, 1887.
    Draws heavily from wartime letters and post-war
narrative of regiment's Colonel to tell regiment's
experiences at South Mountain and Antietam.

440   Wingate, George W. History of the Twenty-Second
Regiment of the National Guard of the State of New York
From its Organization to 1895. New York: Edwin W. Dayton,
1896.

441   Maxon, William. Camp Fires of the Twenty-Third:
Sketches of Camp Life, Marches, and Battles of the
Twenty-Third Regiment, N.Y.V. New York: Davies and Kent,
1863.

442   Fairchild, Charles B., comp. History of the Twenty-
Seventh Regiment, N.Y. Vols. Binghamton: Carl and
Matthews, 1888.
    Based on Fairchild's excellent wartime diary.

443   Boyce, Charles W. A Brief History of the Twenty-Eight
Regiment New York State Volunteers. Buffalo: C.W. Boyce,
1897.
    Text is drawn from the author's diary and official
reports. Latter half contains various articles and
letters from members of the regiment.

444   Judd, David W. The Story of the Thirty-Third New York
State Volunteers: Or, Two Years Campaigning in Virginia
and Maryland. Rochester: Benton and Andrews, 1864.

445   Nash, Eugene. A History of the Forty-Fourth Regiment
New York Volunteer Infantry in the Civil War, 1861-1865.
Chicago: R. R. Donnelly, 1911.

446   Frederick, Gilbert. The Story of A Regiment Being a
Record of the Military Services of the Fifty-Seventh New
York State Volunteer Infantry in the War of the
Rebellion. Chicago: C. H. Morgan, 1895.
        Of limited value on Antietam.

447   Eddy, Richard. History of the Sixtieth Regiment, New
York State Volunteers. Philadelphia: By the Author, 1864.

448   Sharples, Ed. Those Who Took "The Left of the Line": A
History of Company "B," 60th New York Volunteer Infantry
Regiment, October 30th, 1861 to July 17, 1865. n.p., n.d.

449   Root, William Francis S. The Sixty-Ninth Regiment in
Peace and War. New York: Blanchard Press, 1905.

450   Smith, Abram P. History of the Seventy-Sixth Regiment
New York Volunteers. Cortland: Truain, Smith, and Miles
Printers, 1876.
        More useful on South Mountain than Antietam.

451   Fuller, Edward H. Battles of the Seventy-Seventh New
York State Foot Volunteers. n.p., 1901.

452   Todd, William. The Seventy-Ninth Highlanders New York
Volunteers in the War of Rebellion, 1861-1865. Albany:
Brandon, Barton and Co., 1886.
        An above average regimental history, although not as
strong on South Mountain and Antietam as other battles.

453   Gates, Theodore B. The "Ulster Guard" and the War of
the Rebellion. New York: Benjamin H. Tyrrel, 1879.
        The 20th NYSM, or 80th New York. Some fine
information, however, Gates had a tendency to exaggerate
his regiment's accomplishments.

454   Jaques, John W. Three Years: Campaigns of the Ninth
N.Y.S.M. During the Rebellion. New York: Milton and Co.,
1865.
        The 83rd New York. Jaques wartime diary.

455   No Author. History of the Ninth Regiment N.Y.S.M. -
N.G.S.Y.N. New York: Veterans of the Regiment, 1889.
        83rd New York. Some interesting incidents involving
members of the 83rd at Antietam.

456   King, David H., comp. History of the Ninety-Third
Regiment, New York State Volunteer Infantry, 1861-1865.

Milwaukee, WI: Swain & Tate, 1895.
    The 93rd was the headquarter's guard for the Army of
the Potomac.

457   Robertson, Robert S. Personal Recollections of the
War: A Record of Service With the Ninety-Third New York
Volunteer Infantry. Milwaukee: Swain & Tate, 1895.

458   Hall, Isaac. History of the Ninety-Seventh Regiment
New York Volunteers in the War For the Union. Utica: L.
C. Childs, 1890.

459   Kimball, Orville S. History and Personal Sketches of
Company I, One Hundred and Third N.Y.S.V., 1862-1864.
Elmira: Facts Printing Co., 1900.
    Virtually useless for regiment at Antietam.

460   Washburn, George H. A Complete History and Record of
the One Hundred and Eight Regiment N.Y. Vols. From 1862
to 1864. Rochester: E. R. Andrews, 1894.
    A thorough regimental history. Contains many personal
sketches.

461   Clark, James H. The Iron Hearted Regiment: Being an
Account of the Battles, Marches and Gallant Deeds
Performed by the One Hundred and Fifteenth Regiment N.Y.
Vols. Albany: J. Munsell, 1865.
    A Harper's Ferry regiment.

462   Simons, Ezra D. A Regimental History; The One Hundred
and Twenty-Fifth New York State Volunteers. New York: Ezra
D. Simons, 1888.
    A full, though defensive account of the regiment's
participation in the siege and surrender of Harper's
Ferry.

463   Willson, Arabella M. Disaster, Struggle, Triumph. The
Adventures of 1000 "Boys in Blue". Albany: Argus, 1870.
    Highly defensive on regiment's role in Harper's Ferry
siege.

464   Beach, William H. The First New York (Lincoln) Cavalry
From April 17, 1861 to July 7, 1865. New York: The
Lincoln Cavalry Association, 1902.
    Beach was the regimental adjutant. Very full account
of regiment in Maryland.

465   Stevenson, James Hunter. Boots and Saddles: A History
of the First Volunteer Cavalry of the War Known as the
First New York (Lincoln) Cavalry. Harrisburg, PA: Patriot
Publishing Co., 1879.
    Stevenson used his detailed diary to compile this
excellent history.

466   Foster, Alonzo. Reminiscences and Record of the 6th
New York V.V. Cavalry. Brooklyn: 1892.
    Good detail on regiment in Maryland.

467   Hall, Hillman. History of the Sixth New York Cavalry.
Worcester, MA: The Blanchard Press, 1908.

468   Norton, Henry. Deeds of Daring; A History of the
Eighth New York Volunteer Cavalry. Norwich: Chenango Tel.
Printing House, 1889.
    Highly detailed account of the regiment's escape from
Harper's Ferry.

469   _____. A Sketch of the 8th N.Y. Cavalry;
Unwritten History of the Rebellion. Norwich, NY: 1888.

470   Ames, Nelson. History of Battery G, First Regiment New
York Light Artillery. Ann Arbor, MI: University
Microfilms, 1973.

OHIO

471   Ohio, Roster Commission. Official Roster of the
Soldiers of The State of Ohio in the War of the
Rebellion, 1861-1866. 12 vols. Akron: The Werner Company,
1893.

472   Ohio. Antietam Battlefield Commission. Antietam,
Report of the Ohio Antietam Battlefield Commission.
Springfield, OH: Springfield Publishiing Co., 1904.
    Some excellent accounts of Ohio's participation in the
battle.

473   Wilder, Theodore. The History of Company C, Seventh
Regiment, O.V.I. Oberlin: J.B.T. March, 1866.
    Too brief to be of value.

474   Wilson, Lawrence, ed. and comp. Itinerary of the
Seventh Ohio Volunteer Infantry, 1861-1864. New York and
Washington: Neale Publishing, 1907.
    Somewhat disappointing on the 7th at Antietam.

475   Wood, George. The Seventh Regiment: A Record. New
York: James Miller, 1965.
    The best history of the 7th.

476   Sawyer, Franklin. A Military History of the Eighth
Regiment Ohio Vol. Infantry. Cleveland: Fairbanks and
Co., 1881.
    Lacks detail on regiment's operations in Maryland.

477   Horton, Joshua H., comp. A History of the Eleventh
Regiment, Ohio Volunteer Infantry. Dayton: W. J. Shuey,
1866.

More an itinerary of the regiment's travels than a
history.

478   Ward, James E. D. Twelfth Ohio Volunteer Infantry.
Ripley, OH: n.p., 1864.
Some details on South Mountain, otherwise a sketchy
history.

479   Se Cheverell, John H. Journal History of the Twenty-
Ninth Ohio. Cleveland: n.p., 1883.
Author missed Antietam.

480   No Author. History of the Thirty-Second Regiment Ohio
Veteran Volunteer Infantry. Columbus: Cott and Evans,
1896.

481   Kempfer, Lester L. The Salem Light Guard; Company G,
36th Regiment Ohio Volunteer Infantry. Marietta, Ohio,
1861-1865.

PENNSYLVANIA

482   Pennsylvania. Antietam Battlefield Memorial
Commission. Pennsylvania at Antietam. Harrisburg:
Harrisburg Publishing Co., 1906.
Principally orations at monument dedications of 13
different Pennsylvania commands, although there are some
valuable histories of these units at Antietam.

483   _____. Second Brigade of the Pennsylvania
Reserves at Antietam. Harrisburg: Harrisburg Pub. Co.,
1908.
Useful accounts of the four regiments that composed
this brigade.

484   Banes, Charles H. History of the Philadelphia Brigade,
Sixty-Ninth, Seventy-First, Seventy-Second, One Hundred
and Sixth Pennsylvania Volunteers. Philadelphia: J. B.
Lippincott, 1876.
Somewhat disappointing on the brigade's action in the
West Woods.

485   Bates, Samuel P. History of the Pennsylvania
Volunteers, 1861-1865. 5 vols. Harrisburg: B. Singerly,
1870.
Contains the roster and a short history of all
Pennsylvania units.

486   Sypher, Josiah R. History of the Pennsylvania Reserve
Corps. Lancaster: Elias Barr, 1865.
Not a particularly distinguished history. Some useful
details on reserves at South Mountain and Antietam.

487   Cruishank, G. L. Back in the Sixties: Reminiscences of the Service of Co. A, Eleventh Pennsylvania Regiment. Ft. Dodge: Times Job Printing House, 1892.

488   Locke, William H. The Story of the Regiment. Philadelphia: J. B. Lippincott, 1868.
        The 11th Pennsylvania Infantry.

489   Minnigh, Henry N. History of Company K, First Pennsylvania Reserves. Duncanville: "Home Print" Publishers, 1891.
        A typical company history, rather shallow.

490   Woodward, E. M. Our Campaigns; Or, the Marches, Bivouacs, Battles, Incidents of Camp Life and History of Our Regiment During Its Three Years Term of Service. Philadelphia: John E. Potter, 1865.
        The 3d Reserve. Woodward's 1883 history is far superior.

491   Woodward, E. M. History of the Third Pennsylvania Reserve. Trenton: MacCrellish and Quigley, 1883.
        Details on both South Mountain and Antietam.

492   Hardin, Martin D. History of the Twelfth Regiment Pennsylvania Reserve Volunteer Corps. New York: By the Author, 1890.
        Relies heavily upon the Official Records.

493   Glover, Edwin A. Bucktailed Wildcats; A Regiment of Civil War Volunteers. New York: Thomas Yoseloff, 1960.
        The 13th Reserve.

494   Thompson, O. R. Howard, and Rauch, William H. History of the "Bucktails" Kane Rifle Regiment of the Pennsylvania Reserve Corps. Philadelphia: Electric Printing Co., 1906.
        Some good detail on the regiment at both South Mountain and at Antietam on the 16th and 17th.

495   Bobbyshell, Oliver Christian. The Forty-Eighth in the War: Being a Narrative of the Campaigns of the Forty-Eighth Regiment, Infantry, Pennsylvania Veteran Volunteers, During the War of the Rebellion. Philadelphia: Avid Printing Co., 1895.

496   Gould, Joseph. The Story of the Forty-Eight. Philadelphia: Alfred M. Slocum, 1908.
        Most valuable aspect is wartime letters written by brigade commander Nagle, and regimental commander Pleasants.

497   Westbrook, Robert S. History of the Forty-Ninth Pennsylvania Volunteers. Altoona: Altoona Times Print, 1898.

Based upon the diaries of several members of the regiment.

498   Crater, Lewis. History of the Fiftieth Regiment, Penna. Vet. Vols. 1861-1865. Reading: Coleman Printing House, 1884.
        Little of value concerning the Maryland Campaign. See Pennsylvania at Antietam.

499   Parker, Thomas H. History of the Fifty-First Regiment of P.V. and V.V. Philadelphia: King and Baird, 1889.
        Fine, detailed accounts of South Mountain and the fight for Burnside's Bridge.

500   No Author. History of the Sixty-First Regiment Pennsylvania Volunteers 1861-1865. Pittsburgh: Art Engraving and Printing Co., 1911.

501   McDermott, Anthony W. A Brief History of the Sixty-Ninth Regiment Pennsylvania Veteran Volunteers. n.p., n.d.
        Too brief and unreliable.

502   Judson, Amos M. History of the Eighty-Third Pennsylvania Volunteers. Erie: B. F. H. Lynn, 1865.
        A highly observant, entertaining regimental history. Rather thin on participation at Antietam.

503   Vautier, John D. History of the Eighty-Eighth Pennsylvania Volunteers in the War for the Union, 1861-1865. Philadelphia: J. B. Lippincott, 1894.
        Vautier blends personal obervations with an overview of the entire Battle of Antietam. Well worth consulting for Rickett's Division.

504   Mark, Penrose. Red: White: and Blue Badge, Pennsylvania Veteran Volunteers. A History of the 93d Regiment, Known as the "Lebanon Infantry". Harrisburg: Aughinbaugh Press, 1911.
        Fills in some details on the operations of Couch's Division.

505   Uhler, George H. Camps and Campaigns of the 93d Regiment, Penna. Vols. n.p., 1898.

506   Galloway, George Norton. The Ninety-Fifth Pennsylvania Volunteers in the Sixth Corps. Philadelphia: Collins, 1884.
        Of very little value for the Maryland Campaign.

507   Bates, Samuel P. A Brief History of the One Hundredth Regiment. New Castle: W. B. Thomas, 1884.

508   Niebaum, John H. History of the Pittsburgh Washington Infantry 102d Regiment Pennsylvania Veteran Volunteers and Its Forebears. Pittsburgh: Burgum Printing Co., 1931.

509   Ward, Joseph R. C. History of the One Hundred and
Sixth Regiment Pennsylvania Volunteers. Philadelphia: F.
McManus, 1906.
        The best regimental account of the Philadelphia
Brigade's bloody combat in the West Woods with Sedgwick's
Division.

510   Boyle, John Richard. Soldiers True: The Story of the
One Hundred and Eleventh Regiment Pennsylvania Veteran
Volunteers. New York: Eaton and Mains, 1903.
        More concerned with the broader story of the Maryland
Campaign than with the regiment's activities.

511   Peck, H. T. Historical Sketch of the One Hundred and
Eighteenth Regiment Pennsylvania Volunteers. n.p., 1884.

512   No Author. Antietam to Appomattox With the 118th
Penna. Vols., Corn Exchange Regiment. Philadelphia: J. L.
Smith, 1892.
        Outstanding regimental. Numerous personal accounts of
the Battle of Sheperdstown.

513   No Author. History of The Corn Exchange Regiment.
Philadelphia: J. L. Smith, 1888.
        The above is the fuller history.

514   No Author. History of the One Hundred and Twenty-
Fourth Regiment Pennsylvania Volunteers. Philadelphia:
Ware Brothers, 1907.
        Extremely detailed account of the regiment's actions
at Antietam. Includes many personal accounts.

515   No Author. History of the One Hundred and Twenty-
Fifth Regiment Pennsylvania Volunteers, 1862-1863.
Philadelphia: J. B. Lippincott, 1906.
        Another full account with many personal observations.

516   Hays, John. The 130 Regiment, Pennsylvania Volunteers
in the Maryland Campaign and the Battle of Antietam.
Carlisle, Pa.: Herald Printing Co., 1894.
        Much personal detail and observations.

517   No Author. History of the Third Pennsylvania Cavalry,
Sixtieth Pennsylvania Volunteers in the American Civil
War, 1861-1865. Philadelphia: Franklin Print. Co., 1905
        A very complete history.

518   Hyndman, William. History of a Cavalry Company: A
Complete Record of Company "A," Fourth Penna. Cavalry.
Philadelphia: James B. Rodgers, 1870.
        Hardly worth consulting on Maryland Campaign.

519   Kirk, Charles H., ed. and comp. History of the
Fifteenth Pennsylvania Volunteer Cavalry. Philadelphia:
Society of the Fifteenth Pennsylvania Cavalry, 1906.

520   Clark, William, comp. History of Hampton Battery F
Independent Pennsylvania Light Artillery. Akron, O.:
Werner Co., 1909.
        Poor unit history.

521   Guffel, Charles. Durell's Battery in the Civil War.
Philadelphia: Craig, Finley and Co., 1900.
        Contains some excellent original art of Durell's
Battery at Antietam. Good detail on battery's movements
at Antietam.

RHODE ISLAND

522   No Author. Names of Officers, Soldiers and Seamen in
Rhode Island Regiments. Providence Press Co., 1869.

523   Allen, George H. Forty-Six Months With the Fourth
Rhode Island Volunteers, in the War of 1861 to 1865.
Providence, R.I.: J. A. Reid, 1887.
        Excellent. Based upon Allen's wartime journal.

524   Spooner, Henry Joshua. The Maryland Campaign With the
Fourth Rhode Island. Providence, R.I.: The Society, 1903.
        Details of the fight in the 40 acre cornfield on
Burnside's left.

525   Aldrich, Thomas M. The History of Battery A, First
Regiment Rhode Island Light Artillery in the War to
Preserve the Union, 1861-1865. Providence, R.I.: Snow &
Farnham, 1904.
        Some harrowing stories of the battery's service at
Antietam.

526   Reichardt, Theodore. Diary of Battery A, First
Regiment Rhode Island Light Artillery in the War to
Preserve the Union, 1861-1865. Providence, R.I.: Snow &
Farnham, 1904.
        Battery A's day by day wartime experiences. Short
entries.

527   No Author. Battery B, First R.I. Light Artillery.
August 13, 1861 - June 12, 1865. Pawtucket: n.p., 1907.

528   Rhodes, John H. The History of Battery B, First
Regiment Rhode Island Light Artillery. Providence: Snow &
Farnham, 1894.
        An excellent history with much detail.

529   Monroe, John Albert. Battery D First Rhode Island
Light Artillery, at the Battle of Antietam, September 17,
1862. Providence, R.I.: The Society, 1886.
        A detailed account by the battery's commander.

530   Summer, George C. Battery D, First Rhode Island Light
      Artillery, in the Civil War, 1861-1865. Providence: Rhode
      Island Printing Company, 1879.

VERMONT

531   No Author. Vermont in the Civil War. A History of the
      Part Taken by Vermont Soldiers and Sailors. 2 vols.
      Burlington, Vt.: Free Press Association, 1886-1888.
         Contains a good account of Grant's Vermont Brigade at
      Crampton's Gap.

WISCONSIN

532   Love, William Deloss. Wisconsin in the War of the
      Rebellion; A History of All Regiments and Batteries.
      Chicago: Church and Goodman, 1866.

533   Quiner, Edward B. The Military History of Wisconsin: A
      Record of the Civil and Military Patriotism of the State,
      in the War for the Union. Chicago: Clarke and Co., 1866.

534   No Author. Roster of Wisconsin Volunteers, War of the
      Rebellion, 1861-1865. Madison: Democrat Printing Co.,
      1886.

535   Otis, George H. The Second Wisconsin Infantry. Dayton,
      Oh.: Morningside Bookshop, 1984.
         Very brief on 2nd's action at South Mountain and
      Antietam. Also contains William Harries MOLLUS article on
      2d at Antietam.

536   Bryant, Edwin E. History of the Third Regiment of
      Wisconsin Volunteer Infantry, 1861-1865. Madison: Veteran
      Association of the Regiment, 1891.
         Fine regimental. Good description of 3rd's service at
      Antietam. Contains a useful map of 3rd's battle
      movements.

537   Hinkley, Julian Wisner. Narrative of Service With the
      Third Wisconsin Infantry. Madison: Wisconsin History
      Commission, 1912.
         Despite its late date of publication, this is a
      thoroughly reliable and highly detailed memoir.

538   Cheek, Philip and Pointon, Mair. History of the Sauk
      County Riflemen Known as Company "A" Sixth Wisconsin
      Veteran Volunteer Infantry, 1861-1865. ?: By the Author,
      1902.
         One of the better company histories ever published.

539   Dawes, Rufus R. Service With the Sixth Wisconsin
      Volunteers. Marietta, O.: E. R. Alderman, 1890.
         Contains one of the finest first hand descriptions of
      combat at Antietam. A classic, frequently quoted.

8.
Confederate Unit Histories

ARMY LEVEL

540   Wise, Jennings C. The Long Arm of Lee. Lynchburg: J.
P. Bell Co., 1915.
        Although somewhat dated, still the definitive history
of the artillery of the Army of Northern Virginia.

DIVISION LEVEL

541   Schenck, Martin. Up Came Hill; The Story of the Light
Division and Its Leaders. Harrisburg, Pa.: Stackpole Co.,
1958.
        Well written but lightly researched.

BRIGADE LEVEL

542   Cooke, John Esten. Stonewall Jackson and the Old
Stonewall Brigade. Charlottesville: University Press of
Virginia, 1954.

543   Robertson, James I. The Stonewall Brigade. Baton
Rouge: Louisiana State University, 1963.

544   Wilson, John David. George Thomas Anderson's Rebel
Brigade. A Military History, 1861-1865. Ann Arbor:
University Microfilms, 1977.
        Anderson's activities at Antietam are briefly
outlined.

REGIMENTAL LEVEL

ALABAMA

545   Park, Robert Emory. Sketch of the Twelfth Alabama
Infantry of Battle's Brigade, Rodes Division, Early's
Corps, of the Army of Northern Virginia. Richmond, Va.:
W. E. Jones, 1906.
        Barely outlines participation in Maryland.

546   Hurst, M. B. *History of the Fourteenth Regiment
Alabama Vols., With a List of the Names of Every Man That
Ever Belonged to the Regiment*. Richmond: n.p., 1863.
        Similar to Park's history.

547   Oates, William Calvin. *The War Between the Union and
the Confederacy and Its Lost Opportunities, With a
History of the 15th Alabama Regiment and the Forty-Eight
Battles in Which it Was Engaged*. New York: Neal
Publishing Co., 1905.
        Oates missed Antietam, so his treatment is cursory.

548   No Author. *A Sketch of the 47th Alabama Regiment,
Volunteers, C.S.A*. n.p., 1909.
        About one paragraph on the 47th at Antietam.

ARKANSAS

549   Collier, Colvin L. *They'll Do to Tie To*. Little Rock:
Pioneer Press, 1959.
        Poorly researched history of the 3rd Arkansas regiment.

GEORGIA

550   State Division of Confederate Pensions and Records.
Roster of the Confederate Soldiers of Georgia, 1861-1865.
Hapeville, Ga.: Longino and Porter, 1959.

551   Thomas, Henry W. *History of the Doles-Cook Brigade
Army of Northern Virginia C.S.A*. Atlanta: The Franklin
Printing and Publishing Co., 1903.
        Short histories of each regiment that composed this
famous brigade. Also contains many short biographies of
members of the brigade.

552   Lindsay, John W. and Andrews, C. H. *Third Georgia
Regiment, History of its Campaigns, from April 26, 1861
to April 9th, 1865*. Madison, GA: Madisonian, 1890's.

553   Croom, Wendell D. *The War History of Company "C" Sixth
Georgia Regiment*. Fort Valley: "Advertiser" Office, 1879.

554   Austin, Aurelia. *Georgia Boys With "Stonewall"
Jackson, Jones Thomas Thompson and the Walton Infantry*.
Athena: University of Georgia Press, 1967.
        The 11th Georgia.

555   Warren, Kittrell J. *History of the Eleventh Georgia
Volunteers*. Richmond: Smith, Bailey & Co., 1863.
        Brief but with some good detail on the Maryland
Campaign.

556   Willis, Francis T. "The Twelfth Georgia Infantry,"
SHSP, Vol. XVII (1889), pp. 160-187.

A short history of the regiment.

557   Nichols, G. W. A Soldier's Story of His Regiment.
n.p., 1898.
The 61st Georgia. An adequate description of the 61st
at Antietam.

LOUISIANA

558   Commissioner of Military Records. Records of Louisiana
Confederate Soldiers and Louisiana Confederate Commands.
New Orleans: 1920.

559   Owen, William Miller. In Camp and Battle With the
Washington Artillery of New Orleans. Boston: Ticknor and
Co., 1885.
Principally personal recollections. Some valuable
information on the Washington Artillery at Antietam.

MISSISSIPPI

560   Historical Committee. Lamar Rifles; A History of
Company C, Eleventh Mississippi Regiment, C.S.A. Roanoke:
Stone Print. and Mfg. Co., 1903.

561   Brown, Maud. The University Greys, Company A, Eleventh
Mississippi Regiment, Army of Northern Virginia, 1861-
1865. Richmond: Garrett and Massie, 1940.
Little on Antietam.

562   No Author. A Historical Sketch of the Quitman Guards,
Company E. Sixteenth Mississippi Regiment. New Orleans:
Isaac T. Hinton, 1866.

NORTH CAROLINA

563   Clark, Walter. Histories of the Several Regiments and
Battalions from North Carolina in the Great War, 1861-
1865. 5 vols. Raleigh: E. M. Uzell, 1901.
An absolute must for North Carolina regiments. Rich
information on South Mountain, Crampton's Gap, Harper's
Ferry, and Antietam.

564   Manarin, Louis H., comp. North Carolina Troops 1861-
1865. A Roster. 8 +vols. Raleigh: State Department of
Archives and History, 1966.

565   Iobst, Richard W. The Bloody Sixth; The Sixth North
Carolina Regiment, Confederate States of America. Durham:
1965.
Mediocre, modern regimental. Nothing new.

566   Harris, James S. _Historical Sketches, Seventh Regiment North Carolina Troops_. Ann Arbor: University Microfilms, 1972.
        Brief treatment on regiment's services in Maryland.

567   Smith, William Alexander. _The Anson Guards, Company C, Fourteenth Regiment North Carolina Volunteers, 1861-1865_. Charlotte: Stone Pub. Co., 1914.
        Very brief treatment of Antietam.

568   No Author. _History of Company E, 20th N. C. Regiment: 1861-1865_. Ann Arbor: University Microfilms, 1974.

569   Wall, Henry Clay. _Historical Sketch of the Pee Dee Guards (Co. D, Twenty-Third N.C. Regiment) From 1861 to 1865_. Raleigh: Edwards and Broughton, 1876.

570   Graham, James Augustus. "Historical Sketch of the Twenty-Seventh Regiment, North Carolina Infantry," _Our Living and Our Dead_, Vol. I (1874/1875), pp. 97-122.

571   Sloan, John A. _Reminiscences of the Guilford Grays, Co. B, Twenty-Seventh N.C. Regiment_. Washington, D.C.: R. O. Polkinhorn, 1883.

SOUTH CAROLINA

572   Archives Department. _South Carolina Troops in Confederate Service_. Columbia: R. L. Bryan, 1913.
        Never completed all South Carolina rosters.

573   Caldwell. J. F. L. _The History of a Brigade of South Carolinians Known First as "Gregg's" and Subsequently as "McGowan's Brigade."_ Philadelphia: King and Baird, 1866.
        Excellent history. The best unit account of A. P. Hill's Division at Antietam.

574   Dickert, D. Augustus. _History of Kershaw's Brigade_. Newberry: Elbert H. Aull, 1899.
        Another classic. Full account of the brigade at Harper's Ferry and Antietam.

575   Tompkins, D. _Company K, Fourteenth South Carolina Volunteers_. Charlotte, N.C.: Observer, 1897.

576   Edward, W. H. _A Condensed History of Seventeenth Regiment, S.C.V., C.S.A_. Columbia: Press of R. L. Bryan Co., 1908.

TEXAS

577   Polley, Joseph B. _Hood's Texas Brigade: Its Marches, Its Battles, Its Achievements_. New York: Neale Publishing, 1910.

Outstanding. Includes some letters from veterans describing their experiences.

578   Simpson, Harold B. Hood's Texas Brigade: Lee's Grenadier Guard. Waco: Texian Press, 1970.
A well researched "modern" Civil War unit history.

579   Hamilton, D. H. History of Company M, First Texas Volunteer Infantry. Waco: W. M. Morrison, 1962.

580   West, John Camden. A Texan in Search of a Fight. Being the Diary and Letters of a Private Soldier. Waco: S. J. Hill, 1901.
West served in the 4th Texas.

VIRGINIA

581   Loehr, Charles T. War History of The Old First Virginia Infantry Regiment, Army of Northern Virginia. Richmond W. Ellis Jones, 1884.
Very brief history.

582   Robertson, James I. The Fourth Virginia Infantry. Lynchburg: H. E. Howard, 1982.
Part of the "Virginia Regimental Series," a series which will eventually document the activities and provide the roster for every Virginia military unit in the war. New histories are continually being published and this bibliography does not contain all titles. As a rule, the bulk of the book contains the roster. The unit history is generally quite brief.

583   Chamberlaine, William W. Memoirs of the Civil War Between the North and Southern Sections of the United States of America, 1861-1865. Washington, D.C.: Press of B.S. Adams, 1912.
6th Virginia. Valuable description of Battle for Crampton's Gap.

584   Riggs, David F. The 7th Virginia Infantry. Lynchburg: H. E. Howard, 1982.
Virginia Regimental Series.

585   Devine, John E. The 8th Virginia Infantry. Lynchburg: H. E. Howard, 1983.
Virginia Regimental Series.

586   Buck, Samuel. With the Old Confeds. Baltimore: H. E. Houck & Co., 1925.
A good memoir of Buck's service with 13th Virginia.

587   Delaney, Wayne R. The Seventeenth Virginia Volunteer Infantry Regiment, C.S.A. Washington, D.C.: American Printing Co., 1961.

588   Wise, George. History of the Seventeenth Virginia
Infanry, C.S.A. Baltimore: Kelly Piet and Co., 1870.
        Brief narrative of service, but some useful content on
South Mountain and Antietam.

589   Irby, Richard. Historical Sketch of the Nottoway
Grays, Aferwards Company G, Eighteenth Virginia Regiment,
Army of Northern Virginia. Richmond: J. W. Ferguson and
Son, 1878.
        Only touches on Antietam, listing casualties.

590   Wood, William. Reminiscences of Big I. Jackson, Tenn.:
McCowan-Mercer Press, 1956.
        19th Virginia. Wood describes his personal experiences
at South Mountain and Antietam.

591   Wood, James H. The War: "Stonewall: Jackson, His
Campaigns and Battles, The Regiment as I Saw Them.
Cumberland, Md.: Eddy Press, 1910.
        37th Virginia.

592   Krick, Robert K. The 30th Virginia Infantry.
Lynchburg: H. E. Howard, 1983.
        One of the best of the Virginia regimental series.

593   Krick, Robert K. The 40th Virginia Infantry.
Lynchburg: H. E. Howard, 1985.
        Virginia regimental series.

594   Beale, Richard L. T. History of the 9th Virginia
Cavalry, in the War Between the States. Richmond: B. F.
Johnson Publishing, 1899.
        Fine descriptive narrative of a regiment that saw
active service during the Maryland Campaign.

595   Krick, Robert K. The Ninth Virginia Cavalry.
Lynchburg: H. E. Howard, 1982.
        Virginia regimental series.

596   McDonald, William Naylor. A History of the Laurel
Brigade, Originally the Ashby Cavalry of the Army of
Northern Virginia and Chew's Battery. Baltimore: Sun Job
Printing Office, 1907.
        Some information on Munford's Brigade at Crampton's
Gap.

597   Graves, Joseph A. The History of the Bedford Light
Artillery. Bedford City: Press of the Bedford Democrat,
1903.

598   Page, Richard Channing M. Sketch of Page's Battery, or
Morris Artillery, 2d Corps, Army of Northern Virginia.
New York: T. Smeltzer, 1885.

599   Figg, Royall W. "Where only Men Dare to Go!" Or the
Story of a Boy Company C.S.A. Richmond: Whittet and
Sheppem, 1885.
       Contains fine descriptive account of Parker's Battery
at Antietam.

600   Fonerden, Clarence Albert. A Brief History of the
Military Career of Carpenter's Battery. New Market, VA:
Henkel & Co., 1911.

601   Jones, Bejamin W. Under the Stars and Bars; A History
of the Surry Light Artillery. Richmond: E. Waddy, 1909.

602   Krick, Robert Kenneth. Parker's Virginia Battery,
C.S.A. Berryville, VA: Virginia Book Co., 1975.
       A solid, well researched history.

603   Moore, Edward A. The Story of a Cannoneer Under
Stonewall Jackson, in Which is Told the Part Taken by the
Rockbridge Artillery. New York: Neale Publishing, 1907.
       Many personal observations and experiences of campaign
in Maryland.

604   Young, Charles P. "History of Crenshaw's Battery,
Pegram's Battalion, Third Corps, Army of Northern
Virginia," SHSP, Vol. XXXI (1903), pp. 275-296.

9.
Union Leaders
in the Maryland Campaign

605   Palfrey, Francis W. _Memoir of William Francis Bartlett_. Boston: Houghton, Osgood, 1878.
       Memoir of the man whose brigade led the attack at Crampton's Gap.

606   Ballou, Daniel R. _The Military Services of Major-General Ambrose Everett Burnside in the Civil War_. Providence, RI: The Society, 1914.
       General overview of Burnside's military services in the war.

607   Poore, Ben Perley. _The Life and Public Services of Ambrose E. Burnside, Soldier-Citizen-Statesman_. Providence, RI: J. A. and R. A. Reid, 1882.
       Mediocre biography.

608   Woodbury, Augustus. _Ambrose Everett Burnside_. Providence, RI: N. B. Williams, 1882.
       Ignores Burnside's many shortcomings as a soldier.

609   Bower, Jerry Lee. "The Civil War Career of Jacob Dolson Cox." Thesis, Michigan State University, 1970.

610   Schmiel, Eugene David. "The Career of Jacob Dolson Cox, 1828-1900: Soldier, Scholar, Statesman." Thesis, Ohio State University, 1969.

611   Ambrose, Stephen A. _Halleck: Lincoln's Chief of Staff_. Baton Rouge: Louisiana State University Press, 1962.
       Well researched and written biography. Might give Halleck more credit than he is due.

612   Forney, John W. _Life and Military Career of Winfield Scott Hancock_. Philadelphia: Hubbard, 1880.

613   Freed, A. T. Hancock: The Life and Public Services of
Winfield Scott Hancock. Chicago: Henry A. Summer, 1880.

614   Hancock, Anne. Reminiscences of Winfield Scott
Hancock. New York: Charles L. Webster, 1887.
      Not very useful.

615   Tucker, Glenn. Hancock The Superb. New York: D.
Appleton, 1897.
      Still the best biography of Hancock, but shallow
research.

616   Walker, Francis A. General Hancock. New York: D.
Appleton, 1897.
      Walker served on Hancock's staff during the war.

617   Walker, Francis A. Hancock in the War of the
Rebellion. New York: G. J. Little & Co., 1891.
      Walker was a staff officer in Hancock's 2d Corps.

618   No Author. In Memorium - Major General George L.
Hartstuff, Class of 1852. Norwood, Mass.: Press of
Charles G. Wheelock, 1875.

619   Herbert, Walter H. Fighting Joe Hooker. Indianapolis,
Ind.: Bobbs-Merrill, 1944.
      Suffers from depth of research.

620   Shanks, W. F. G. "Fighting Joe Hooker," Harpers New
Monthly Magazine. n.d.

621   Achorn, Edgar O. Major General Oliver Otis Howard.
Cumberland Gap, TN: Lincoln Memorial University, 1910.
      Rare.

622   Carpenter, John A. "An Account of the Civil War Career
of Oliver Otis Howard Based on His Private Letters."
Thesis, Columbia University, 1954.

623   _____,_____. Sword and Olive Branch: Oliver Otis
Howard. Pittsburg, PA: University of Pittsburgh Press,
1964.
      A fine biography, well researched and written.

624   Longacre, Edward G. The Man Behind the Guns: A
Biography of General Henry Jackson Hunt, Chief of
Artillery, Army of the Potomac. South Brunswick, NJ: A.
S. Barnes, 1977.
      A solid biography. Well documented.

625   Curtis, George Ticknor. Life, Character, and Public
Services of General George B. McClellan. Boston:
Cupplies, Upham, 1887.
      An address on McClellan. Hero-worship material.

626   Hassler, Warren W.,Jr. General George B. McClellan:
Shield of the Union. Baton Rouge: Louisiana State
University Press, 1957.
        Pro-McClellan. Ignores many of his failings and shifts
blame for many of McClellan's woes on others.

627   Hillard, G. S. Life and Campaigns of George B.
McClellan, Maj. Gen. U.S.A. Philadelphia: J. B.
Lippincott, 1865.
        Too close to the war to have many details beyond
official sources.

628   Hurlbert, William Henry. General McClellan and the
Conduct of the War. New York: Sheldon, 1864.

629   Mayhew, Lewis B. "George B. McClellan Reevaluated."
Thesis, Michigan State College of Agriculture and Applied
Science, 1952.

630   Michie, Peter S. General McClellan. New York: D.
Appleton, 1901.
        The best study of McClellan's military career. Even-
handed and written by a soldier of high regard.

631   Sears, Stephen W. George B. McClellan: The Young
Napoleon. New York: Ticknor and Fields, 1988.
        The most well-written and researched biography of
McClellan's entire life available.

632   Swinton, William. McClellan's Military Career Reviewed
and Exposed: The Military Policy of the Administration
Set Forth and Vindicated. Washington, D. C.: Lemuel
Towers, 1864.
        Swinton attempts to further damage McClellan's
military reputation.

633   Wilkes, George. McClellan: Who He Is and What He Has
Done and Little Mac: "From Ball's Bluff to Antietam." New
York: The American News Company, 1864.

634   Williams, T. Harry. McClellan, Sherman and Grant. New
Brunswick, NJ: Rutgers University Press, 1962.
        A distinquished historian compares three great
leaders.

635   Bache, Richard Meade. Life of General George G. Meade,
Commander of the Army of the Potomac. Philadelphia: Henry
T. Coates & Co., 1897.

636   Cleaves, Freeman. Meade of Gettysburg. Norman, OK:
University of Oklahoma Press, 1960.

637   Lyman, Theodore. Meade's Headquarters, 1863-1865:
Letters of Colonel Theodore Lyman From the Wilderness to
Appomattox. Boston: The Atlantic Monthly Press, 1922.
        The best insight into Meade's personality and
character available. An outstanding book.

638   Meade, George G., Jr. Life and Letters of George
Gordon Meade. 2 vols. New York: Charles Scribner's Sons,
1913.
        Contains several letters Meade wrote to his wife
describing his service in the Maryland Campaign.

639   Miles, Nelson A. Serving the Republic: Memoirs of the
Civil and Military Life of Nelson A. Miles. New York:
Harper's & Brothers, 1911.
        Very brief on his service with 61st and 64th New York
at Antietam.

640   Sparks, David., ed. Inside Lincoln's Army: The Diary
of General Marsena Rudolph Patrick, Provost-Marshall
General, Army of the Potomac. New York: Thomas Yoseloff,
1964.
        A mine of information. Very detailed on both South
Mountain and Antietam.

641   Sedgwick, Henry D., comp. Correspondence of John
Sedgwick, Major General. 2 vols. ?: DeVinnie Press, 1902.
        Contains Sedgwick's limited, but interesting, Maryland
Campaign correspondence.

642   Winslow, Richard E. General John Sedgwick, the Story
of a Union Corps Commander. Novato, CA: Presido Press,
1982.
        A well done biography. Contains some useful
information on Sedgwick at Antietam.

10.
Confederate Leaders in the Maryland Campaign

643   Kline, Maurice Nickell. _Edward Porter Alexander_.
Athens: University of Georgia Press, 1971.

644   Elliott, Joseph Cantey. _Lieutenant General Richard
Heron Anderson. Lee's Noble Soldier_. Dayton, OH:
Morningside, 1985.
       Rather brief on Maryland Campaign but does contain
some previously untapped information about Anderson.

645   Early, Jubal A. _Autobiographical Sketch and Narrative
of the War Between the States_. Philadelphia: J. B.
Lippincott, 1912.
       Early made few friends with this volume. It is
quite valuable for the Maryland Campaign.

646   Gordon, John. _Reminiscences of the Civil War_. New
York: Charles Scribners Sons, 1904.
       Although possibly embellished, Gordon's description of
the defense of the "sunken lane" is memorable. Ignores
South Mountain.

647   Tankersly, Allen P. _John B. Gordon: A Study in
Gallantry_. Atlanta: Whitehall Press, 1955.
       Offers little beyond Gordon's own reminiscences
concerning Antietam.

648   Wellman, Manly Wade. _Giant in Gray: A Biography of
Wade Hampton of South Carolina_. New York: Charles
Scribners, 1949.

649   Hassler, William W. _A. P. Hill: Lee's Forgotten
General_. Richmond: Garrett and Massie, 1957.
       Although splendidly written, rather thinly researched.

650   Schenck, Martin. _Up Came Hill: The Story of the Light
Division and of Its Leaders_. Harrisburg: Stackpole, 1958.
       Much like above. Well written, light research.

651   McMurray, Richard Mannning. John Bell Hood and the War
for Southern Independence. Lexington: University Press of
Kentucky, 1982.
A fine biography of this aggressive soldier.

652   Chambers, Lenoir. Stonewall Jackson. 2 Vols. New York:
William Morrow, 1959.
An outstanding biography. Thorough discussion of
Jackson's role in the Maryland Campaign.

653   Cooke, John Esten. The Life of Stonewall Jackson From
Official Papers, Contemporary Narrative, and Personal
Acquantance. New York: C. B. Richardson, 1863.
Useful principally for Cooke's personal acquaintance
of Jackson.

654   Dabney, R. L. Life and Campaigns of Lieut. - Gen.
Thomas J. Jackson. New York, Blalock, 1866.
Dabney was Jackson's Chief of Staff through the Seven
Days Battles. Many interesting insights.

655   Davis, Burke. They Called Him Stonewall; A Life of Lt.
General T. J. Jackson, C.S.A. New York: Rinehart, 1954.
For younger readers.

656   Henderson, G. F. R. Stonewall Jackson and the American
Civil War. 2 Vols. New York: Longmans, Green, 1906.
Fine biography. Excellent military anaylsis.

657   Davis, Burke. Gray Fox; Robert E. Lee and the Civil
War. New York: Rinehart, 1956.
Like Davis' book on Jackson.

658   Dowdy, Clifford and Manarin, Louis H., eds. The
Wartime Papers of R. E. Lee. Boston: Little, Brown, &
Co., 1961.

659   Dowdy, Clifford. Lee. Boston: Little, Brown & Co.,
1965.
A piercing, well written one volume biography of Lee.

660   Freeman, Douglas S. R. E. Lee: A Biography. 4 Vols.
New York: Charles Scribners Sons, 1934.
A classic work and still the most exhaustive
biography of Lee.

661   Lee. Robert E, Jr. Recollections and Letters of
General Robert E. Lee. Garden City: Garden City
Publishing Co., 1924.
Nothing of interest concerning Antietam.

662   Hattaway, Herman Morrell. General Stephen D. Lee.
Jackson: University Press of Mississippi, 1976.
Useful for Lee's service at Antietam.

663   Eckenrode, H. J. and Conrad, Bryan. _James Longstreet,_
Lee's War Horse. Chapel Hill: University of North
Carolina Press, 1936.
         A fair, even-handed biography, although out-dated.

664   Sanger, Donald Bridgeman. _General James Longstreet and_
the Civil War. Chicago: University of Chicago Literaries,
1937.
         Poorly researched and unreliable.

665   Lee, Susan. _Memoirs of William Nelson Pendleton_.
Philadelphia: J. B. Lippincott, 1893.

666   Holtzman, Robert S. _Adapt or Perish: The Life of_
General Roger A. Pryor, C.S.A. Hamden, CT: Archon Books,
1976.

667   McClellan, H. B. _I Rode With Jeb Stuart_. Bloomington,
IN: Indiana University Press, 1958.

668   _____,_____. _The Life and Campaigns of Major-_
General J. E. B. Stuart. New York: Houghton Mifflin,
1885.
         More a history of the campaigns of Stuart's cavalry
than a biography of his life. Highly useful for Stuart's
operations in Maryland.

11.
General Histories

669   Catton, Bruce. Mr. Lincoln's Army. New York:
Doubleday, 1962.
      Part of the trilogy of the Army of the Potomac.
Extremely readable account of Antietam but lightly
documented. Fine appraisal of McClellan.

670   _____,_____. Terrible Swift Sword. Garden City,
NY: Doubleday, 1961-65.
      Beautifully written. Well documented. Addresses
political as well as military outcome and purpose of
Maryland Campaign.

671   Coffin, Charles Carleton. Drum-Beat of the Nation: The
First Period of the War of the Rebellion From Its
Outbreak to the Close of 1862. New York: Harper and
Brothers, 1902.
      Written by a correspondent who reported the war. Not
altogether reliable. Northern bias.

672   Commager, Henry Steele, ed., The Blue and the Gray:
The Story of the Civil War as Told by the Participants. 2
Vols. Indianapolis: Bobbs-Merrill, 1950.
      Some good, but well-known Antietam accounts.

673   Congdon, Don, ed. Combat: The Civil War. New York:
Delacorte Press, 1967.
      Like Commager's volume, good accounts selected, but
well known.

674   Foote, Shelby. The Civil War: A Narrative. 3 Vols.
New York: Random House, 1958-1974.
      Well written, but no footnotes.

675   Johnson, Robert U., and Buel, Clarence C., ed.,
Battles and Leaders of the Civil War. 4 Vols. New York:
Century, 1887.
      Compilation of the outstanding articles that appeared
in Century Magazine, from privates to generals. Volume 2
concerns Maryland Campaign.

676   McPherson, James. <u>Battle Cry of Freedom</u>. New York:
Oxford University Press, 1988.
       Called the best single volume history of the Civil
War. Useful for political analysis of Maryland Campaign.

677   Nevins, Allan. <u>The War for the Union</u>. 3 Vols. New
York: Charles Scribners Sons, 1959-1971.
       A highly distinguished work.

678   Paris, Louis Philippe Albert D'Orleans. <u>History of the
Civil War in America</u>. 4 vols. New York: Holmes and Meier,
1875-1888.
       An English translation of the Comte de Paris' history.
A fair, even-handed history of the war.

679   Pollard, Edward Alfred. <u>Southern History of the War:
The Second Year of the War</u>. New York: C. B. Richardson,
1863.
       Distinctly biased and inaccurate in many details.

680   Randall, J. G. and Donald, David. <u>The Civil War and
Reconstruction</u>. Boston: D. C. Heath, 1961.
       One of the best single volume histories of the war.

681   Rhodes, James Ford. <u>History of the Civil War, 1861-
1865</u>. New York: Macmillan Co., 1917.

682   Ropes, John Codman. <u>The Story of the Civil War; a
Concise Account of the War in the United States of
America Between 1861 and 1865</u>. G.P. Putnam: New York and
London, 1894-1913.
       Volume two concerns the Maryland Campaign. A study of
strategy and operations. Well-balanced, incisive, and
judicious in its criticism.

683   Starr, Stephen Zoltan. <u>The Union Cavalry in the Civil
War</u>. 3 Vols. Baton Rouge: Louisiana State University
Press, 1979-1985.
       Has become the standard work on Union cavalry in the
war. Full explanation of the problems of Union cavalry in
the Maryland Campaign.

684   Swinton, William. <u>Campaigns of the Army of the
Potomac</u>. New York: C. Scribner's Sons, 1892.
       A critical analysis by a former war correspondent.
Highly useful interpretation.

685   _____, _____. <u>The War for the Union. The First,
Second, Third, and Fourth Years of the War</u>. New York:
Loyal Publication Society, 1864.
       Distinctly northern bias.

686   Williams, Kenneth P. <u>Lincoln Finds a General</u>. 5 vols.
Macmillan: New York, 1949-59.
       Volume two concerns the Maryland Campaign. A
fascinating analysis but flawed by overreliance on the

Official Records and an unreasonable contempt for
McClellan.

687   Williams, T. Harry. <u>Lincoln</u> <u>and</u> <u>His</u> <u>Generals</u>. New York
Alfred A. Knopf, 1952.
Useful in understanding the Lincoln-McClellan
relationship during the Maryland Campaign.

688   Wolseley, Garnet Joseph. <u>The</u> <u>American</u> <u>Civil</u> <u>War,</u> <u>An</u>
<u>English</u> <u>View</u>. Charlottsville, VA: University Press of
Virginia, 1964.
A British Lieutenant Colonel and observer of the war,
Wolseley's account is an interesting, detached view of the
war.

12.
The Order of Battle:
Army of the Potomac

GENERAL HEADQUARTERS

Major General George B. McClellan

FIRST ARMY CORPS

Major General Joseph Hooker (W)
Brig. Gen. George G. Meade

FIRST DIVISION

Brigadier General John P. Hatch (W)
Brigadier General Abner Doubleday

FIRST BRIGADE   SECOND BRIGADE

Col. Walter Phelps, Jr.   Brig. Gen. Marsena Patrick

22d   New York   21st New York
24th New York   23d New York
30th New York   35th New York
84th New York (14th Brooklyn)   80th New York (20th
2d   U.S. Sharpshooters   Militia)

THIRD BRIGADE	FOURTH BRIGADE
Brig. Gen. Abner Doubleday Colonel William Wainwright (W) Lt. Colonel J. William Hoffman	Brig. Gen. John Gibbon

7th Indiana 76th New York 95th New York 56th Pennsylvania	19th Indiana 2d Wisconsin 6th Wisconsin 7th Wisconsin

ARTILLERY

New Hampshire Light, First Battery
1st Rhode Island Light, Battery D
1st New York Light, Battery L
4th United States, Battery B

SECOND DIVISION

Brigadier General James B. Ricketts

FIRST BRIGADE	SECOND BRIGADE
Brig. Gen. Abram Duryea	Col. William Christian Col. Peter Lyle
97th New York 104th New York 105th New York 107th Pennsylvania	26th New York 94th New York 88th Pennsylvania 90th Pennsylvania

THIRD BRIGADE

Brig. Gen. George L. Hartstuff (W)
Col. Richard Coulter

16th Maine (detached Sept. 13)
12th Massachusetts
13th Massachusetts
83rd New York
11th Pennsylvania

ARTILLERY

1st Pennsylvania Light, Battery F
Pennsylvania Light, Battery C

THIRD DIVISION

Brig. Gen. George G. Meade
Brig. Gen. Truman Seymour

FIRST BRIGADE

Brig. Gen. Truman Seymour
Col. R. Biddle Roberts

1st Pennsylvania Reserves
2d   Pennsylvania Reserves
5th Pennsylvania Reserves
6th Pennsylvania Reserves
13th Pennsylvania Reserves

SECOND BRIGADE

Col. Albert L. Magilton

3d Pennsylvania Reserves
4th Pennsylvania Reserves
7th Pennsylvania Reserves
8th Pennsylvania Reserves

THIRD BRIGADE

Col. Thomas F. Gallagher (W)
Lt. Col. Robert Anderson

9th Pennsylvania Reserves
10th Pennsylvania Reserves
11th Pennsylvania Reserves
12th Pennsylvania Reserves

ARTILLERY

1st Pennsylvania Light, Battery A
1st Pennsylvania Light, Battery B
5th United States, Battery C

SECOND ARMY CORPS

Major General Edwin V. Sumner

FIRST DIVISION

Major General Israel B. Richardson (MW
Brig. Gen John C. Caldwell
Brig. Gen Winfield Hancock

FIRST BRIGADE

Brig. Gen. John C. Caldwell

5th New Hampshire
7th New York
61st New York
64th New York
81st Pennsylvania

SECOND BRIGADE

Brig. Gen Thomas Meagher
Col. John Burke

29th Massachusetts
63d New York
69th New York
88th New York

THIRD BRIGADE

Col. John R. Brooke

    2d   Delaware
    52d   New York
    57th New York
    66th New York
    53d   Pennsylvania

ARTILLERY

1st New York Light, Battery B
4th U. S., Batteries A and C

SECOND DIVISION

Major General John Sedgwick (W)
Brig. Gen. Oliver O. Howard

FIRST BRIGADE   SECOND BRIGADE

Brig. Gen. Willis A. Gorman   Brig. Gen Oliver O. Howard
                                     Col. Joshua Owen
15th Massachusetts
1st Minnesota   69th Pennsylvania
34th New York   71st Pennsylvania
82d New York   72d Pennsylvania
Massachusetts Sharpshooters,   106th Pennsylvania
 1st Co.
Minnesota Sharpshooters,
 2d Co.

THIRD BRIGADE

Brig. Gen. Napoleon J. T. Dana (W)
Col. Norman J. Hall

    19th Massachusetts
    20th Massachusetts
    7th Michigan
    42d New York
    59th New York

ARTILLERY

1st Rhode Island, Battery A
1st United States, Battery I

THIRD DIVISION

Brig. Gen. William H. French

FIRST BRIGADE

Brig. Gen Nathan Kimball

14th Indiana
8th Ohio
132d Pennsylvania
7th West Virginia

SECOND BRIGADE

Col. Dwight Morris

14th Connecticut
108th New York
130th Pennsylvania

THIRD BRIGADE

Brig. Gen. Max Weber (W)
Col. John W. Andrews

1st Delaware
5th Maryland
4th New York

ARTILLERY

1st New York Light, Battery G
1st Rhode Island Light, Battery B
1st Rhode Island Light, Battery G

FOURTH ARMY CORPS

Maj. Gen Darious N. Couch

FIRST BRIGADE

Brig. Gen. Charles Devens, Jr.

7th Massachusetts
10th Massachusetts
36th New York
2d Rhode Island

SECOND BRIGADE

Brig. Gen. Albion P. Howe

62d New York
93d Pennsylvania
98th Pennsylvania
102d Pennsylvania
139th Pennsylvania

THIRD BRIGADE

Brig. Gen. John Cochrane

65th New York
67th New York
122d New York
23d Pennsylvania
61st Pennsylvania
82d Pennsylvania

ARTILLERY

New York Light, Third Battery
1st Pennsylvania Light, Battery C
1st Pennsylvania Light, Battery D
2d Unites States, Battery G

FIFTH ARMY CORPS

Maj. Gen. Fitz John Porter

FIRST DIVISION

Maj. Gen. George W. Morell

FIRST BRIGADE

Col. James Barnes

2d	Maine
18th	Massachusetts
22d	Massachusetts
1st	Michigan
13th	New York
25th	New York
118th	Pennsylvania

Massachusetts Sharpshooters,
 2d Co.

SECOND BRIGADE

Brig. Gen Charles Griffin

2d	District of Columbia
9th	Massachusetts
32d	Massachusetts
4th	Michigan
14th	New York
62d	Pennsylvania

THIRD BRIGADE

Col. T. B. W. Stockton

20th Maine
16th Michigan
12th New York
17th New York
44th New York
83d Pennsylvania
Massachusetts Sharpshooters, Brady's Co.

ARTILLERY

Massachusetts Light, Battery C
1st Rhode Island Light, Battery C
5th United States, Battery D

SECOND DIVISION

Brig. Gen. George Sykes

FIRST BRIGADE   SECOND BRIGADE

Lt. Col. Robert C. Buchanan   Maj. Charles S. Lovell

3d U.S.   1st and 6th U.S.
4th U.S.   2d and 10th U.S.
12th U.S., 1st Battalion   11th U.S.
12th U.S., 2nd Battalion   17th U.S.
14th U.S., 1st Battalion
14th U.S., 2nd Battalion

THIRD BRIGADE

Col. Gouverneur K. Warren

5th New York
10th New York

ARTILLERY

1st United States, Batteries E and G
5th United States, Battery I
5th United States, Battery K

THIRD DIVISION

Brig. Gen. Andrew A. Humphreys

FIRST BRIGADE   SECOND BRIGADE

Brig. Gen. Erastus B. Tyler   Col. Peter H. Allabach

91st Pennsylvania   123rd Pennsylvania
126th Pennsylvania   131st Pennsylvania
129th Pennsylvania   133d Pennsylvania
134th Pennsylvania   155th Pennsylvania

ARTILLERY

1st New York Light, Battery C
1st Ohio Light, Battery L

ARTILLERY RESERVE

1st Battalion New York Light, Battery A
1st Battalion New York Light, Battery B
1st Battalion New York Light, Battery C
1st Battalion New York Light, Battery D
New York Light, Fifth Battery
1st United States, Battery K
4th United States, Battery G

SIXTH ARMY CORPS

Maj. Gen. William B. Franklin

FIRST DIVISION

Maj. Gen. Henry W. Slocum

FIRST BRIGADE	SECOND BRIGADE
Co. Alfred T. A. Torbert	Col Joseph Bartlett
1st New Jersey	5th Maine
2d New Jersey	16th New York
3d New Jersey	27th New York
4th New Jersey	96th Pennsylvania

THIRD BRIGADE

Brig. Gen. John Newton

18th New York
31st New York
32d New York
95th Pennsylvania

ARTILLERY

Maryland Light, Battery A
Massachusetts Light, Battery A
New Jersey Light, Battery A
2d United States, Battery D

SECOND DIVISION

Brig. Gen. William F. Smith

FIRST BRIGADE	SECOND BRIGADE
Brig. Gen. Winfield Hancock	Brig. Gen. W. T. H. Brooks
Col. Amasa Cobb	
	2d Vermont
6th Maine	3d Vermont
43d New York	4th Vermont
49th Pennsylvania	5th Vermont
137th Pennsylvania	6th Vermont
5th Wisconsin	

THIRD BRIGADE

Col. William H. Irwin

7th Maine

```
                    20th New York
                    33d  New York
                    49th New York
                    77th New York
```

ARTILLERY

```
        Maryland Light, Battery B
        New York Light, 1st Battery
        5th United States, Battery F
```

NINTH ARMY CORPS

```
        Maj. Gen. Ambrose Burnside
        Maj. Gen. Jesse Reno (K)
        Brig. Gen. Jacob Cox
```

FIRST DIVISION

```
        Brig. Gen. Orlando Willcox
```

FIRST BRIGADE	SECOND BRIGADE
Col. Bejamin C. Christ	Col. Thomas Welsh
28th Massachusetts	8th Michigan
17th Michigan	46th New York
79th New York	45th New York
50th Pennsylvania	100th Pennsylvania

ARTILLERY

```
    Massachusetts Light, Eighth Battery
    2d United States, Battery E
```

SECOND DIVISION

```
        Brig. Gen. Samuel D. Sturgis
```

FIRST BRIGADE	SECOND BRIGADE
Brig. Gen. James Nagle	Brig. Gen. Edward Ferrero
2d Maryland	21st Massachusetts
6th New Hampshire	35th Massachusetts
9th New Hampshire	51st New York
48th Pennsylvania	51st Pennsylvania

ARTILLERY

```
        Pennsylvania Light, Battery D
        4th United States, Battery E
```

THIRD DIVISION

Brig. Gen Isaac P. Rodman

FIRST BRIGADE	SECOND BRIGADE
Col. Harrison Fairchild	Col. Edward Harland
9th New York	8th Connecticut
89th New York	11th Connecticut
103d New York	16th Connecticut
	4th Rhode Island

ARTILLERY

5th United States, Battery A

FOURTH DIVISION

Brig. Gen. Jacob Cox
Brig. Gen. Eliakim P. Scammon

FIRST BRIGADE	SECOND BRIGADE
Col. Eliakim P. Scammon	Col. George Crook
Col. Hugh Ewing	
12th Ohio	11th Ohio
23rd Ohio	28th Ohio
30th Ohio	36th Ohio
Ohio Light Artillery,	Schambeck's Co. Chicago
1st Battery	Dragoons
Gilmore's Co. West Virginia	Kentucky Light Artillery
Cavalry	
Harrison's Co. West Virginia	
Cavalry	

UNATTACHED

6th New York Cavalry
Ohio Cavalry, 3d Independent Co.
3d U. S. Artillery, Batteries L and M

TWELFTH ARMY CORPS

Maj. Gen. Joseph Mansfield (MW)
Brig. Gen. Alpheus Williams

FIRST DIVISION

Brig. Gen Alpheus Williams
Brig. Gen. Samuel W. Crawford (W)
Brig. Gen. George H. Gordon

FIRST BRIGADE

Brig. Gen. Samuel Crawford
Col. Joseph F. Knipe

5th   Connecticut(detached)
10th   Maine
28th   New York
46th   Pennsylvania
124th Pennsylvania
125th Pennsylvania
128th Pennsylvania

SECOND BRIGADE

Brig. Gen. George H. Gordon

27th Indiana
 2d Massachusetts
13th New Jersey
107th New York
Zouaves d'Afrique
3d Wisconsin

SECOND DIVISION

Brig. Gen. George S. Greene

FIRST BRIGADE

Lt. Col. Hector Tyndale
Maj. Orrin Crane

 5th Ohio
 7th Ohio
29th Ohio
66th Ohio
28th Pennsylvania

SECOND BRIGADE

Col. Henry Stainrook

 3d Maryland
102d New York
109th Pennsylvania
111th Pennsylvania

THIRD BRIGADE

Col. William Goodrich (K)
Lt. Col. Jonathan Austin

3d Delaware
Purnell Legion
60th New York
78th New York

ARTILLERY

Maine Light, 4th Battery
Maine Light, 6th Battery
1st New York Light, Battery M
New York Light, 10th Battery
Pennsylvania Light, Battery E
Pennsylvania Light, Battery F
4th United States, Battery F

CAVALRY DIVISION

Brig. Gen. Alfred Pleasonton

FIRST BRIGADE	SECOND BRIGADE
Maj. Charles J. Whiting	Col. Richard Rush
5th United States 6th Unites States	4th Pennsylvania 6th Pennsylvania

THIRD BRIGADE	FOURTH BRIGADE
Col. John Farnsworth	Col. A. T. McReynolds
8th Illinois 3d Indiana 1st Massachusetts 8th Pennsylvania	1st New York 12th Pennsylvania

FIFTH BRIGADE

Col. Benjamin F. Davis

8th New York
3d Pennsylvania

ARTILLERY

2d United States, Battery A
2d United States, Battery B and L
2d United States, Battery M
3d United States, Batteries C and G

UNATTACHED

1st Maine Cavalry
12th Pennsylvania Cavalry (detachment)

13.
The Order of Battle:
Army of Northern Virginia

General Robert E. Lee

LONGSTREET'S CORPS

Maj. Gen. James Longstreet

McLaws' Division

Maj. Gen. Lafayette McLaws

KERSHAW'S BRIGADE	SEMMES' BRIGADE
Brig. Gen. Joseph B. Kershaw	Brig. Gen Paul Semmes
2d South Carolina	10th Georgia
3d South Carolina	53d Georgia
7th South Carolina	15th Virginia
8th South Carolina	32d Virginia

COBB'S BRIGADE	BARKSDALE'S BRIGADE
Brig. Gen. Howell Cobb	Brig. Gen. Wm. Barksdale
Lt. Col. C. C. Sanders	
Lt. Col. William MacRae	13th Mississippi
	17th Mississippi
16th Georgia	18th Mississippi
24th Georgia	21st Mississippi
Cobb's Legion (GA)	
15th North Carolina	

ARTILLERY

Manly's (NC) Battery
Pulaski (GA) Artillery
Richmond (Fayette) Artillery
Richmond Howitzers (1st Co.)
Troup (GA) Artillery

ANDERSON'S DIVISION

Maj. Gen. Richard H. Anderson (W)
Brig. Gen. Roger Pryor

WILCOX'S BRIGADE

Col. Alfred Cumming

8th   Alabama
9th   Alabama
10th Alabama
11th Alabama

ARMISTEAD'S BRIGADE

Brig. Gen. L. A. Armistead
Col. J. G. Hodges

9th   Virginia
14th Virginia
38th Virginia
53d   Virginia
57th Virginia

MAHONE'S BRIGADE

Col. William Parham

6th   Virginia
12th Virginia
16th Virginia
41st Virginia
61st Virginia

PRYOR'S BRIGADE

Brig. Gen. Roger Pryor

14th Alabama
2d   Florida
8th   Florida
3d   Virginia

FEATHERSTON'S BRIGADE

Brig. Gen. W. S. Featherston
Col. Carnot Posey

12th Mississippi
16th Mississippi
19th Mississippi
 2d   Mississippi Battalion

WRIGHT'S BRIGADE

Brig. Gen. A. R. Wright

44th Alabama
3d   Georgia
22d   Georgia
48th Georgia

ARTILLERY

Donaldsonville (LA) Artillery
Huger's (VA) Battery
Moorman's (VA) Battery
Grime's (VA) Battery

JONES DIVISION

Brig. Gen. David R. Jones

TOOMBS' BRIGADE

Brig. Gen. Robert Toombs
Col. Henry L. Benning

2d   Georgia
15th Georgia
17th Georgia
20th Georgia

DRAYTON'S BRIGADE

Brig. Gen. T. F. Drayton

50th Georgia
51st Georgia
15th South Carolina

PICKETT'S BRIGADE

Brig. Gen. Richard Garnett

8th Virginia
18th Virginia
19th Virginia
28th Virginia
56th Virginia

KEMPER'S BRIGADE

Brig. Gen. James L. Kemper

1st Virginia
7th Virginia
11th Virginia
17th Virginia
24th Virginia

JENKINS' BRIGADE

Col. Joseph Walker

1st South Carolina
2d South Carolina
5th South Carolina
6th South Carolina
4th South Carolina Batt.
Palmetto (SC) Batt.

ANDERSON'S BRIGADE

Col. Geo. T. Anderson

1st Georgia (Regulars)
7th Georgia
8th Georgia
9th Georgia
11th Georgia

ARTILLERY

Wise (VA) Artillery

WALKER'S DIVISION

Brig. Gen. John G. Walker

WALKER'S BRIGADE

Col. Van H. Manning
Col. E. D. Hall

 3d Arkansas
27th North Carolina
46th North Carolina
48th North Carolina
30th Virginia
French's (VA) Battery

RANSOM'S BRIGADE

Brig. Gen. Robt. Ransom

24th North Carolina
25th North Carolina
35th North Carolina
49th North Carolina
Branch's (VA) Artillery

HOOD'S DIVISION

Brig. Gen. John B. Hood

HOOD'S BRIGADE

Col. W. T. Wofford

18th Georgia
Hampton (SC) Legion
1st Texas
4th Texas
5th Texas

LAW'S BRIGADE

Col. E. M. Law

4th Alabama
2d Mississippi
11th Mississippi
6th North Carolina

ARTILLERY

German (SC) Artillery
Palmetto (SC) Artillery
Rowan (NC) Artillery

EVANS BRIGADE

Brig. Gen. Nathan G. Evans
Col. P. F. Stevens

17th South Carolina
18th South Carolina
22d South Carolina
23d South Carolian
Holcombe (SC) Legion
Macbeth (SC) Artillery

CORPS ARTILLERY

WASHINGTON (LA) ARTILLERY

Col. J. B. Walton

1st Co.
2d Co.
3d Co.
4th Co.

LEE'S BATTALION

Col. S. D. Lee

Ashland (VA) Artillery
Bedford (VA) Artillery
Brooks (SC) Artillery
Eubank's (VA) Battery
Madison (LA) Artillery
Parker's (VA) Battery

JACKSON'S CORPS

Maj. Gen. Thomas J. Jackson

EWELL'S DIVISION

Brig. Gen. A. R. Lawton (W)
Brig. Gen. Jubal A. Early

LAWTON'S BRIGADE

Col. M. Douglass (K)
Maj. J. H. Lowe
Col. John H. Lamar

13th Georgia
26th Georgia
31st Georgia
38th Georgia
60th Georgia
61st Georgia

TRIMBLE'S BRIGADE

Col. James A. Walker

15th Alabama
12th Georgia
21st Georgia
21st North Carolina
1st North Carolina Batt.

EARLY'S BRIGADE

Brig. Gen. Jubal A. Early
Col. Wm. Smith

13th Virginia
25th Virginia
31st Virginia
44th Virginia
49th Virginia
52d Virginia
58th Virginia

HAYS' BRIGADE

Brig. Gen. Harry T. Hays

5th Louisiana
6th Louisiana
7th Louisiana
8th Louisiana
14th Louisiana

ARTILLERY

Charlottesville (VA) Artillery
Chesapeake (MD) Artillery
Courtney (VA) Artillery
Johnson's (VA) Battery
Louisiana Guard Artillery
1st Maryland Battery
Staunton (VA) Artillery

HILL'S LIGHT DIVISION

Maj. Gen. Ambrose P. Hill

BRANCH'S BRIGADE

Brig. Gen. L. O'B. Branch(K)
Col. James H. Lane

7th North Carolina
18th North Carolina
28th North Carolina
33d North Carolina
37th North Carolina

ARCHER'S BRIGADE

Brig. Gen. J. J. Archer

5th Alabama Batt.
19th Georgia
1st Tennessee
7th Tennessee
14th Tennessee

GREGG'S BRIGADE

Brig. Gen. Maxcy Gregg

1st South Carolina
1st South Carolina Rifles
12th South Carolina
13th South Carolina
14th South Carolina

PENDER'S BRIGADE

Brig. Gen. Dorsey Pender

16th North Carolina
22d North Carolina
34th North Carolina
38th North Carolina

FIELD'S BRIGADE

Col. J. Brockenbrough

40th Virginia
47th Virginia
55th Virginia
22d Virginia Batt.

THOMAS' BRIGADE

Col. Edward L. Thomas

14th Georgia
35th Georgia
45th Georgia
49th Georgia

ARTILLERY

Branch (NC) Artillery
Crenshaw's (VA) Battery
Fredricksburg (VA) Artillery
Letcher (VA) Artillery
Middlesex (VA) Artillery
Pee Dee (SC) Artillery
Purcell (VA) Artillery

JACKSON'S DIVISION

Brig. Gen. John. R. Jones
Col. A. J. Grigsby

WINDER'S BRIGADE

Col. A. J. Grigsby

2d   Virginia
4th Virginia
5th Virginia
27th Virginia
33d Virginia

JONES' BRIGADE

Col. B. T. Johnson

21st Virginia
42d Virginia
48th Virginia
1st Virginia Batt.

TALIAFERRO'S BRIGADE

Col. E. T. H. Warren

47th Alabama
48th Alabama
10th Virginia
23d Virginia
37th Virginia

STARKE'S BRIGADE

Brig. Gen. Wm. Starke(K)
Col. L. A. Stafford

1st Louisiana
2d Louisiana
9th Louisiana
10th Louisiana
15th Louisiana
Coppens' (LA) Batt.

ARTILLERY

Alleghany (VA) Artillery
Brockenbrough's (MD) Battery
Danville (VA) Artillery
Hampden (VA) Artillery
Lee (VA) Battery
Rockbridge (VA) Artillery

HILL'S DIVISION

Maj. Gen. Daniel H. Hill

RIPLEY'S BRIGADE	GARLAND'S BRIGADE
Brig. Gen. Roswell Ripley(W) Col. George Doles	Brig. Gen. S. Garland (K) Col. D. K. McRae
4th Georgia 44th Georgia 1st North Carolina 3d North Carolina	5th North Carolina 12th North Carolina 13th North Carolina 20th North Carolina 23d North Carolina

RODES' BRIGADE	ANDERSON'S BRIGADE
Brig. Gen. Robert E. Rodes	Brig. Gen. G. B. Anderson Col. R. T. Bennett
3d Alabama 5th Alabama 6th Alabama 12th Alabama 26th Alabama	2d North Carolina 4th North Carolina 14th North Carolina 30th North Carolina

COLQUITT'S BRIGADE

Col. Alfred H. Colquitt

13th Alabama
6th Georgia
23d Georgia
27th Georgia
28th Georgia

ARTILLERY

Hardaway's (Al) Battery
Jeff Davis (AL) Artillery
Jones' (VA) Battery
King William (VA) Artillery

RESERVE ARTILLERY

BROWN'S BATTALION	JONES' BATTALION
Powhatan Artillery Richmond Howitzers, 2d Co. Richmond Howitzers, 3d Co. Salem Artillery Williamsburg Artillery	Morris (VA) Artillery Orange (VA) Artillery Turner's (VA) Battery Wimbish's Battery

CUTT'S BATTALION

Blackshears' (GA) Battery
Irwin (GA) Artillery
Lloyd's (NC) Battery
Patterson's (GA) Battery
Ross' (GA) Battery

NELSON'S BATTALION

Amherst (VA) Artillery
Fluvanna (VA) Artillery
Huckstep's (VA) Artillery
Johnson's (VA) Battery
Milledge (GA) Artillery

MISCELLANEOUS

Cutshaw's (VA) Battery
Dixie (VA) Artillery
Magruder (VA) Artillery

CAVALRY DIVISION

Maj. Gen. James E. B. Stuart

HAMPTON'S BRIGADE

Brig. Gen. Wade Hampton

1st North Carolina
2d   South Carolina
10th Virginia
Cobb's (GA) Legion
Jeff. Davis Legion

LEE'S BRIGADE

Brig. Gen. Fitz Lee

1st Virginia
3d Virginia
4th Virginia
5th Virginia
9th Virginia

ROBERTSON'S BRIGADE

Col. Thomas Munford

2d   Virginia
6th Virginia
7th Virginia
12th Virginia
17th Virginia Batt.

HORSE ARTILLERY

Chew's (VA) Battery
Hart's (SC) Battery
Pelham's (VA) Battery

Index

CPSIA information can be obtained
at www.ICGtesting.com
Printed in the USA
JSHW030758050422
24470JS00002BA/48

9 780313 280719